CW01368631

SPITFIRE

AIR WORLD

SPITFIRE
The Iconic Fighter in Unique Photographs

First published in Great Britain in 2025 by
Air World
An imprint of
Pen & Sword Books Ltd
Yorkshire – Philadelphia

Copyright © Dilip Sarkar, 2025

ISBN 978 1 03614 691 7

The right of Dilip Sarkar to be identified as Author of this work has been asserted by him in accordance with the Copyright, Designs and Patents Act 1988. A CIP catalogue record for this book is available from the British Library All rights reserved.

All rights reserved. No part of this book may be reproduced, transmitted, downloaded, decompiled or reverse engineered in any form or by any means, electronic or mechanical including photocopying, recording or by any information storage and retrieval system, without permission from the Publisher in writing. NO AI TRAINING: Without in any way limiting the Author's and Publisher's exclusive rights under copyright, any use of this publication to 'train' generative artificial intelligence (AI) technologies to generate text is expressly prohibited. The Author and Publisher reserve all rights to license uses of this work for generative AI training and development of machine learning language models.

Typeset by SJmagic DESIGN SERVICES, India.
Printed and bound in the UK by CPI Group (UK) Ltd.

The Publisher's authorised representative in the EU for product safety is Authorised Rep Compliance Ltd., Ground Floor, 71 Lower Baggot Street,
Dublin D02 P593, Ireland.
www.arccompliance.com

For a complete list of Pen & Sword titles please contact:

PEN & SWORD BOOKS LTD
George House, Units 12 & 13, Beevor Street, Off Pontefract Road,
Barnsley, South Yorkshire, S71 1HN, England
E-mail: enquiries@pen-and-sword.co.uk
Website: www.pen-and-sword.co.uk

or

PEN AND SWORD BOOKS,
1950 Lawrence Road, Havertown, PA 19083, USA
E-mail: uspen-and-sword@casematepublishers.com
Website: www.penandswordbooks.com

MIX
Paper | Supporting responsible forestry
FSC® C013604

SPITFIRE

THE ICONIC FIGHTER IN UNIQUE PHOTOGRAPHS

DILIP SARKAR
MBE FRHistS FRAeS

AIR WORLD

Contents

Prologue vi

Spitfire: The Photographic Kaleidoscope 1

Reflections 122

Acknowledgements 124

Select Bibliography 125

Other Books by Dilip Sarkar 126

Prologue

'A Real Killer Fighter' at War

In the psyche of the British public, the Supermarine Spitfire was a winner from the outset. This was not just because of its stunning sleek lines, elliptical wing and high performance, but because the Spitfire was a direct descendant from Supermarine's famous Schneider Trophy winning British seaplane racers. This spectacular competition took place between 1919 and 1931, aircraft racing at low-level over water, providing a breathtaking spectacle for spectators, the competition becoming one of great national pride accelerating aircraft design. To push performance boundaries, aircraft designers began breaking away from the traditional fabric-covered biplane, instead producing faster, metal-covered, monoplanes – and at the forefront of these exciting developments was Supermarine's chief designer, Reginald Joseph Mitchell – who would go on to use the experience gained when designing the Spitfire.

In 1927, Mitchell's S5 achieved first and second place, setting a new air speed record of 281.66 mph. In 1929, the improved S6 won again, with an average speed of 328.63 mph. Afterwards, the S6 was confirmed as the fastest and most technologically advanced aircraft in the world when Squadron Leader Orlebar set a new world record at 357.7 mph. Britain needed one more consecutive victory to permanently retain the coveted silver trophy but the Wall Street Crash dictated the withdrawal of government funding for the next race. An eccentric patriot, Lady Houston, incensed at the prospect of Britain being unable to compete, then wrote a cheque for £100,000 – enabling Mitchell to win the Schneider Trophy in 1931 with the S6B's staggering 340.08 mph.

PROLOGUE

In spite of the seaplane's high performance and the patriotic fervour generated by the race, the RAF's Air Member for Supply and Research, Air Vice-Marshal Hugh Dowding, considered the racing seaplanes useless for military purposes. Nonetheless, Dowding did appreciate the clear superiority of monoplanes, leading to the issue of Air Ministry Specification F7/30 on 1 October 1931, inviting private tenders from aircraft designers to produce a new fighter for the RAF. As Dowding said, 'I wanted to… cash in on the experience gained in aircraft construction and engine progress'.

And that is how the Spitfire story began.

The requirements for F7/30 were:

1. Highest possible rate of climb.
2. Highest possible speed at 15,000 feet.
3. Fighting view.
4. Manoeuvrability.
5. Capability of ease and rapid production in quantity.
6. Ease of maintenance.

The Air Ministry also required the new fighter's maximum speed to be at least 250 mph, and carry four machine guns. Surprisingly, Gloster Aircraft won the competition with a radial-engined biplane, the SS37, although this never entered production. Fortunately, though, the Air Ministry recognised that the design's edge in performance was insufficient, considering the speeds new German fighters and bombers were achieving, meaning that it would soon become obsolete. At Supermarine, Mitchell had found F7/30 'too restrictive … to produce an aircraft of the highest possible performance'. Consequently, Supermarine and aero-manufacturer Rolls-Royce decided to privately collaborate on a 'real killer fighter'. The Air Ministry was notified of this and advised that under no circumstances would any official interference be tolerated. In November 1934, therefore, Mitchell began work on his 'Type 300 Fighter'.

A month later, the Air Ministry commissioned Supermarine to produce an 'improved F7/30 design', from which point the project became government funded. On 3 January 1935, Supermarine confirmed this arrangement and provided details of their new machine. This specification included all the

F7/30 requirements in addition to a tail wheel, as opposed to the more traditional skid, and wing-mounted machine guns firing beyond the propeller arc. Whilst this work was in progress, in April 1935 the Air Ministry redefined its requirement for the new 'Single-Engine Single-Seater Day and Night Fighter' in F10/35. The main points were:

1. Had to be at least 40 mph faster than contemporary bombers at 15,000 feet.
2. 'Have a number of forward firing machine-guns that can produce the maximum hitting power possible in the shortest space of time available for one attack'. The Air Ministry 'considered that eight guns should be provided'.
3. Had to achieve 'the maximum possible and not less than 310 mph at 15,000 feet at maximum power with the highest speed possible between 5,000 and 15,000 feet'.
4. Have the best possible climbing performance to 20,000 feet, although this was considered of secondary importance to 'speed and hitting power'.
5. Be armed with at least six but preferably eight machine-guns, all forward firing and wing mounted outside the propeller arc. These were to be fired by 'electrical means'. In the event of six guns being used, 400 rounds per gun was necessary, 300 if eight were fitted.
6. Had to be 'a steady firing platform'.
7. Had to include the following 'special features' and equipment:
   a) Enclosed cockpit.
   b) Cockpit heating.
   c) Night flying equipment.
   d) Radio Telephony (R/T).
   e) Oxygen for two-and-a-half hours.
   f) Easily accessed and maintained guns.
   g) Retractable undercarriage and tail wheel.
   h) Wheel brakes.

Such an aircraft would indeed be a 'real killer fighter'. Interestingly, however, the Air Staff did not dictate that it must be a monoplane, indicating that monoplanes were not yet considered supreme in the corridors of Whitehall.

PROLOGUE

A study in 1932 had concluded that more guns were required to destroy a modern bomber, hence why the new RAF fighters would have eight machine guns. It was believed that the new breed of monoplane fighters would be so fast as to permit their pilots just one pass: the more guns brought to bear, therefore, for those few seconds the better. The choice of the .303 rifle-calibre Browning gun would prove a mistake, however. Bitter experience in the early stage of the Second World War indicated that a heavier projectile was much better, and preferably a cannon shell. Nevertheless, the new specification and thought process reflected progress.

In 1933, Adolf Hitler and the Nazis came to power in Germany, the clouds of war quickening over Europe thereafter. The following year, the RAF's annual air exercise was a fiasco, only two of the five bombers engaged in a mock attack being intercepted. Incredibly, Britain's air defences at the time were incapable of dealing with more than five raiders simultaneously. Indeed, the prevalent air doctrine of the day was entirely focused on the bomber delivering a knock-out blow, meaning that the emphasis of production and development was focused on the bomber force. The year before Hitler became chancellor, in fact, the British Prime Minister Stanley Baldwin told the House of Commons that 'the bomber would always get through' and that 'the only defence is offence, meaning that you have to kill more woman and children more quickly than the enemy if you want to save yourselves'. Air Chief Marshal Sir Hugh Trenchard, the 'Father of the RAF', agreed, stating in 1921 that the aeroplane 'was a shockingly bad weapon for defence', and that the use of fighters was justified only 'to keep up the morale of your own people'. Defence spending, therefore, was effectively side-lined and provided only the bare minimum of resources. So little was spent on re-armament, in fact, that Winston Churchill described the years 1931–1935 as those of 'the locust'. By 1935, though, it was clear that although Germany was unlikely to be ready for war until 1939, Hitler's preparations were so advanced that the threat could no longer be ignored. Consequently, at last, Britain began to re-arm. In August 1936, German forces were deployed to Spain, fighting on behalf of the fascist General Franco, providing Hitler with an opportunity to test new weapons and tactics. On 27 April 1936, German bombers caused great damage to and loss of civilian life at Guernica – emphasising to many

Baldwin's ominous prediction. Others, including Dowding – fortunately soon to play a key role in the air defence of Britain – disagreed, believing that the fighter was an essential weapon. Challenging Trenchard's policy, Dowding argued that unless the home base could be adequately protected against enemy bombers, it would be impossible for the bomber force to deliver a knock-out or counter blow against the enemy. Ultimately events would prove him right: but it was clear now that, in any case, the RAF desperately needed its new 'killer fighter'.

Mitchell's first design, the Type 224, was unsuccessful, however, which is actually why the Hawker Hurricane fighter, designed by Sydney Camm, flew before the Spitfire and became available in large numbers quicker than the Spitfire. Mitchell knew, in fact, that time was running out on two counts: firstly, and obviously, the threat from Nazi Germany, and secondly because, having been diagnosed with rectal cancer, he was dying. Not knowing whether fate would provide him sufficient time to complete the project, Mitchell continued working on the Type 300. The result – the Supermarine Spitfire, so-called after Supermarine's chairman's nickname for his daughter – was immediately striking, akin to a winged bullet, elliptical wings providing a unique signature. The prototype, K5054, first flew from Southampton's Eastleigh airfield on 5 March 1936. This twenty minute test flight was entirely successful. On 3 June 1936, the Air Ministry ordered 310 Spitfires at a cost of £4,500 each (excluding engine, guns, instruments and radios). It was expected that the first Spitfires would be delivered to the RAF in October 1937, but it soon became apparent that Supermarine – a small company of only 500 employees – lacked the capacity to fulfil large orders. Eventually, the first Spitfire was delivered on 19 July 1938. Tragically, Mitchell himself had not lived to see the moment: this brilliant aircraft designer died, aged 42, on 11 June 1937. On 4 August 1938, Supermarine Test Pilot Jeffrey Quill delivered the first operational aircraft, K9789, to 19 Squadron at Duxford, which was equipped with obsolete Gloster Gauntlet biplanes at that time. Flight Sergeant George Unwin took one look at the new, monoplane and decided that 'this was the fighter I wanted to go to war with. It was a decision I never had occasion to regret.'

PROLOGUE

Hawker's Hurricane fighter had first flown on 6 November 1935, 111 Squadron receiving the first production Hurricane in November 1937. It has often been argued that because Camm's design relied upon traditional construction techniques, as opposed to the all metal, monocoque construction of the Spitfire, it was easier to produce and henceforth why the Air Ministry initially ordered more Hurricanes than Spitfires. That may to some extent be so, but the Hurricane's lack of a metal-covered wing was a design deficiency, taking some time to rectify. This is an early indication that the Hurricane was inferior not only to the Spitfire but – much more ominously – Germany's Me 109. Professor Willy Messerschmitt's 'Augsburg Eagle' was the first of the three fighters to fly, in May 1935.

The new German monoplane fighter had been designed around the concept of the smallest, and therefore lightest, airframe around the most powerful engine. This featured a metal-alloy framework, flush-riveted stressed metal covering, leading-edge wing slots in conjunction with slotted trailing-edge flaps, which increased the wing area upon demand, retractable undercarriage and a jettisonable canopy. The 109 was initially armed with two nose-mounted 7.92 mm machine guns, and, like the original Hurricanes and Spitfires, a wooden fixed pitch propeller. Blooded during the Spanish Civil War, the 109 set a new world speed record of 379.38 mph. This unprecedented speed was achieved because of the aircraft's new Daimler-Benz 601 engine. Spitfires and Hurricanes were both powered by the Rolls-Royce Merlin engine, the Mk III variant of which, during the Battle of Britain ahead, being more powerful than the DB601A at all altitudes. The German engine, however, had one great advantage: it was fuel injected and therefore unaffected by gravity, negative-g causing the Merlin's float-type carburettor to cut out momentarily in the dive, meaning that the 109 could always outpace a Spitfire in that attitude. The 109's fixed-pitch propeller was soon replaced by the three-bladed VDM 'controllable pitch' airscrew, permitting rotation of the blades through 360°, enabling the selection of the optimum setting for any situation. The British fighters were first updated to the de Havilland two-pitch propeller – fine pitch for take-off, coarse for flight. Although the British were developing their Constant Speed (CS) propeller, which was comparable to the VDM unit, this would not be fitted to all RAF fighters until 16 August 1940 – during the Battle of Britain itself – increasing the Spitfire's rate of climb by 730 feet per minute.

In respect of fighter armament, the Germans initially lagged behind the British. News that the new RAF fighters were armed with eight machine guns led to a rapid re-think. The difficulty was that the 109's wings were so thin that it could not carry more than two guns. The effect of a further pair of machine guns was really inconsequential, so it was decided to wing-mount two 20 mm MG-FF Oerlikon cannons. This weapon's muzzle velocity was much lower than a machine gun: eight rounds per second to the machine gun's seventeen. Regardless, there was no comparison between the destructive power of a puny machine-gun bullet and a fist-sized cannon shell – just one strike from such a round could prove fatal. Machine guns, though, provide a spread-effect, much like a shot gun, and are therefore more suited to the average shot, rather than exceptional marksman; this combination of both machine gun and cannon gave the Germans the best of both worlds. Although a circumstance arrived at more by accident than intention, this too would prove immeasurably advantages in the early battles ahead.

After the Munich Crisis of 1938, Hitler became increasingly confident and became focused on an aggressive expansionist policy. Even so, many believed that Hitler was merely rectifying what were seen as various injustices imposed upon Germany by the Versailles Peace Treaty of 1919, but the violent events of 1 September 1939 indicated the *Führer*'s true intentions: Germany invaded Poland. Hitler ignored an ultimatum from Britain and France to withdraw his troops immediately, and so, with a heavy heart, the British prime minister, Neville Chamberlain – who had personally worked indefatigably to appease the Nazi dictator and avoid another world war – broadcast to the British people on 3 September 1939 that the country was at war with Nazi Germany. The time had come for Supermarine's 'real killer fighter' to prove its worth in anger.

In 1936, RAF Fighter Command had been created with responsibility for the air defence of Britain. The country was divided into four fighter groups and the British Isles were surrounded by an invisible ring of radar beams, providing early warning of an enemy air attack. The chief and creator of this System of Air Defence was none other than the former Air Member

PROLOGUE

for Supply and Development, now Air Chief Marshal Sir Hugh Dowding. At the outbreak of war, however, the fighter scenario was not entirely optimistic. Fighter Command possessed 16 squadrons of Hurricanes – some 497 aircraft – 11 of which remained at home, whilst four went to France with the Advance Air Striking Force. Only 187 Spitfires were operational, just 11 squadrons in total, all of which were retained for home defence. It is often argued that the opposing air forces were numerically equally matched, which may be so, but some stark statistics require consideration to correctly appreciate the situation Dowding faced. In addition to their Spitfires and Hurricanes, Fighter Command also had fifteen other fighter squadrons. The fact is, though, that eight of these were flying obsolete Gloster Gladiator biplanes, and seven the twin-engined Bristol Blenheim Mk IF. The latter would ultimately prove useless as a day fighter, as did its enemy counterpart the Me 110, and be related to night fighting. It was only, therefore, the twenty-seven Hurricane and Spitfire that mattered so far as a daylight contest was concerned. Against this force was ranged 850 operational Me 109s (supplemented by 195 Me 110s).

Before war came in 1939, Fighter Command had no point of reference so far as devising tactics for the new monoplane fighters was concerned. There were several factors to consider. Firstly, and significantly, it was wrongly believed that due to the high speeds achieved by this new generation of fighters, fighter-to-fighter combat like in the First World War, would be impossible. The human body, they thought, would simply be unable to cope with the high levels of negative-g and other physical strains imposed by high speed manoeuvres. Moreover, the range of fighters, being short-range defensive machines, is limited (Spitfire Mk I: 395 miles, Hawker Hurricane Mk I: 505 miles and Me 109E: 412 miles). Given the distance between Britain and Germany, any intrusion over British air space was expected to be by longer-range bombers, and, indeed, small formations of them. Twin-engined bombers, being slower and less manoeuvrable than single-engined fighters, were considered easy to shoot down – especially if the RAF fighters were closely bunched together and operating in concert, so as to simultaneously bring multiple guns to bear. The standard Fighter Command formation became the 'vic' of three aircraft, the squadron of twelve being sub-divided into such sections. Each section could attack with twenty-four guns in a single pass – against an enemy bomber which was expected to obligingly continue straight and level, taking little or no evasive action. Each section would attack successively, raking the target with a total of ninety-six machine guns. The involvement of enemy fighters was not a consideration in this scenario, their limited range restricting their activities to defending their own nation's air space – not engaging in long-range offensive operations.

Certainly the experience of RAF pilots during 1939 and early 1940 gave no indication of how wrong the Fighter Command tacticians would ultimately be proved in due course. Although the anticipated and immediate attempt at a 'knock-out blow' by the *Luftwaffe* failed to materialise, it was indeed only German bombers that were active over England. On 16 October 1939, the first air attack on Britain took place when thirty Ju 88s of I/KG 30 attacked British shipping in the Firth of Forth. At 3.30 pm, Flight Lieutenant George Pinkerton of 602 Squadron scored the Spitfire's first aerial victory by shooting down one of these raiders which crashed into the sea off Port Seton. Such enemy raids continued, as did Spitfire successes against them. On 21 October the Hurricane recorded its first combat successes, when three mine-laying He 115 seaplanes were shot down off Yorkshire by 46 Squadron. Enemy bombers were also destroyed over France by Hurricanes – and so, for the first few months following the outbreak of war, what Flight Lieutenant Brian Lane described as a 'queer war' continued, with still no sign of the dreaded 'knock-out' blow. Again ominously, however, the Air Ministry concluded that 'There is no doubt that by 1939 the Me 109 was superior to any Allied fighter except the Spitfire, which, however, was then only available to the RAF in small numbers'. Fortunately in the months that followed, British aircraft production began exceeding German output, and as Spitfire production stepped up, via a system of sub-contracting, more of Mitchell's 'real killer fighter' reached the squadrons – but would it be enough?

On 26 March 1940 the RAF destroyed its first Me 109. This was not achieved by a Spitfire, however: because Spitfire squadrons were based entirely at home, it was only the Hurricanes in France that had such an opportunity. On that day, 73 Squadron engaged enemy fighters over

PROLOGUE

Saarlautern and Trier, claiming four destroyed and two unconfirmed. On 9 April 1940 the 'Phoney War' ended abruptly when Germany invaded Norway. Although a British task force was rapidly despatched, the Royal Navy (RN) failed to prevent a successful enemy seaborne landing. Naturally this increased Dowding's concern for the defence of Britain, and emphasised the importance of preserving his small fighter force for home defence. On 2 May 1940 a comparison took place between a captured Me 109 and a Hurricane. The 109 was found to be up to 40 mph faster but unable to out-turn the Hawker fighter. It was also evident that unless the Hurricane was rapidly fitted with a CS propeller, it would continue to be at a significant performance disadvantage.

By this time, the superiority of *Luftwaffe* fighter tactics was also evident. These had been worked out in Spain, and relied upon three things: height, sun and a tactical formation known as the *Schwärm*. Unlike their RAF counterparts, the Germans had actual combat experience with the Me 109, and realised very quickly that aircraft should be spread out, unlike the RAF 'vic'. Maintaining a respectable distance between aircraft of around 200 metres, the enemy pilots did not have to concentrate on formation flying, but could instead search for the enemy. Further, the German fighters flew in a line abreast formation and in a section of four, the aircraft occupying the positions of an outstretched hand's fingertips. The foremost aircraft was the section leader. The extreme left aircraft was the leader's wingman, the position being reversed for the right-hand pair. In combat the *Schwärm* broke into these two fighting pairs, the leader's job being to attack, covered by his wingman. Another crucial factor was the 109's superior service ceiling (36,000 feet) compared to the Hurricane and Spitfire Mk Is (34,000 feet). Height, enabling a fighter leader to position himself between the enemy and the dazzling sun, achieved surprise: and surprise was everything.

On 10 May 1940 Hitler attacked the West, German forces invading Belgium, Holland, Luxembourg and France. Airborne troops and motorised infantry, supported by tanks and aircraft operating as flying artillery, isolated, enveloped and paralysed the Allies. The tragedy of the Fall of France has often been told, so it is unnecessary to re-visit that narrative here. The crucial thing for our purposes is that Dowding refused to send Spitfires to France and waste them on an already lost battle, this being further evidence of the Spitfire's superiority. The catastrophic events in France, however, coupled with the total absence of any attempt by the German bombers to administer a 'knock-out' blow on Britain were throwing British air power experts into confusion. Over the battlefields of France the Me 109 achieved complete aerial superiority, enabling German ground forces to operate unhindered by RAF air attacks. John Terraine has rightly argued that a strong and appropriately equipped Allied fighter force was the only thing capable of preventing this. The Germans had given the Allies a devastating lesson in the benefit of possessing and correctly deploying a modern fighter force. From this point onwards it was clear that the bomber orientated air doctrine of the between-the-wars period was completely flawed. In a nutshell, Trenchard was wrong, Dowding, thankfully as future events would further prove, was right. Suddenly the fighter aircraft achieved a level of usefulness and potency hitherto unconsidered by the British.

By 26 May 1940, the British Expeditionary Force (BEF) had no alternative but to retire on and be evacuated from the Channel port of Dunkirk. The story of this operation, codenamed Dynamo, is well-known and has a special place in the British popular memory of the Second World War. The fact remains, however, that the BEF had suffered high casualties and left behind all armour and heavy equipment. Although the British propaganda machine hailed Dunkirk as a victory, and there can be no doubt that the rescue of 340,000 troops was a welcome deliverance, it is as well to remember that wars are not won by evacuations. It was during the appended protective air operation that the Spitfire met the Me 109 for the first time. Until now, Dowding had preserved his precious Spitfires for home defence, but so hard-pressed had the Hurricane squadrons been in France that he was now forced to commit Spitfires to the battle raging across the Channel. There was a high-risk factor involved, given that Dunkirk lay 50 miles across the sea from 11 Group's closest airfields; this meant two sea crossings per patrol and, of course, any contact was likely to be over the French coast. Spitfires shot down were likely, therefore, to crash into the sea or perhaps crash-land in France, resulting in the capture of pilots. Those who bailed out into the sea faced the prospect of rescue with uncertainty, given that formal air sea rescue arrangements

PROLOGUE

were woefully inadequate or non-existent. The operation was placed in the capable hands of Air Vice-Marshal Keith Park, commander of 11 Group. The Spitfire force available amounted to just sixteen squadrons, meaning that the provision of a constant fighter umbrella over the Dunkirk beaches during daylight was impossible. All Fighter Command could do was its best under difficult circumstances. Ironically, therefore, the Spitfire's first real test came not as a short-range defensive interceptor, but an offensive fighter operating at a range well beyond that envisaged by Mitchell. Fortunately at this time, Fighter Command's pilots were given one performance advantage: 100 octane fuel, significantly improving the Merlin's boost and aircraft's rate of climb. Emergency boost, of + 12 lbs per square inch could be used in an emergency, to get a pilot either quickly to action or out of trouble, but only for a few minutes. Spitfire pilots fighting over Dunkirk would often be thankful for this expedient.

The first big air battle between the opposing fighter forces took place over Calais on 23 May 1940. The Spitfires of 54 Squadron claimed three 109s destroyed, 92 Squadron two. The balance sheet at close of play was unfavourable to Fighter Command, however: seven Spitfires had been destroyed and ten pilots lost in total. As the operation continued, the air fighting increased intensified. As the days wore on Park began operating his squadrons in multiples of four, although, largely due to communication difficulties and because such a scenario was unpredicted, these did not operate as a 'wing', in the way that comparable formations did from 1941 onwards. It was more a case of squadrons travelling across the sea in convoy, arriving over the French coast together and in numbers. Once battle was joined, though, the formations completely lost cohesion. As the Spitfire pilots gained in experience daily, the Germans soon developed a grudging respect for the Spitfire, described in the *Luftwaffe War Diaries* as possessing a comparable performance to the Me 109E. Indeed, over the French coast at least, the balance of power shifted completely in the Spitfire pilots' favour – and for the purposes of the evacuation below, that was where it mattered at that desperate time. Certainly Park considered that his force had achieved 'total ascendency' over the German bombers, and that 'the Spitfire performed very well at Dunkirk'. Moreover, the deficiencies highlighted in

RAF tactical doctrine, techniques and procedures could be improved in time for the coming Battle of Britain.

Following the conclusion of the Dunkirk evacuation at the beginning of June 1940, a lull ensued until the night of 18/19 June 1940, when some seventy He 111 bombers intruded over East Anglia – and the Spitfire recorded its first nocturnal victory. Neither the Hurricane or Spitfire, however, were created as night-fighters, and the Spitfire in particular, due to its narrow track undercarriage and glowing banks of exhausts blinding the pilot's night vision, was never a great night flyer. Nonetheless, so unprepared were Britain's night-time defences that the experiment to use both types after dark was justified. At 12.30 am that night, the South African Flight Lieutenant A.G. 'Sailor' Malan of 74 Squadron destroyed a He 111 near Chelmsford, followed by another forty-five minutes later. Such nocturnal successes, however, proved rare.

France formally surrendered on 22 June 1940. There followed a further lull, as both sides retired to take stock. On 27 June, experimental cannon-armed Spitfires were delivered to 19 Squadron at Fowlmere in the Duxford Sector of 12 Group. The fighting over France had highlighted the advantages of the 109's 20-mm cannon, an omission Fighter Command needed to swiftly address. The Me 109's wing section is extremely thin, but German engineers had accommodated the Oerlikon's ammunition drum by fitting blisters to the upper and under wing surfaces. Surprisingly, given that captured 109s had been examined, this the Air Ministry did not do. The 20-mm Hispano Suiza cannon was side-mounted, so as to be accommodated by the Spitfire's wing section. Shells were belt-fed from boxes, instead of the intended drum, but in combat, as the wing flexed, stoppages occurred as shell cases jammed upon ejection. This Spitfire, the Mk IB, was only armed with two cannon, so if one or both weapons jammed the pilot was not only obliged to break off any action but was extremely vulnerable. During most of the summer ahead, this problem would continue to vex 19 Squadron, as a solution was sought. Some squadrons previously engaged over Dunkirk also recognised the impracticality of Fighter Command's stipulated tactics, and so began many *ad hoc* experiments by certain squadron commanders to devise their own preferred formations.

PROLOGUE

The occupation of France by the enemy changed everything, so far as the defence of Britain was concerned. The vital importance of aerial superiority over the battlefield had been demonstrated to shocking effect by the *Luftwaffe* fighters over France. Operating from bases in Northern France, even London was now within range of the Me 109. Although the 109's limited fuel capacity provided only twenty minutes flying time over the British capital, this meant that London was at great risk of daylight attack by German bombers. Far from being alone or in small groups, as the Fighter Command tacticians originally expected, the enemy bombers could now be escorted by large numbers of Me 109s – all the way to London and back. As Winston Churchill, who had replaced Chamberlain as prime minister on 10 May, told the nation: 'The Battle of France is over. I expect that the Battle of Britain is about to begin.'

The Battle of Britain's bibliography is enormous, and it is not my intention to provide a narrative here. Instead I would refer readers to my eight-volume, 1 million-word, narrative, being the official history produced for The Battle of Britain Memorial Trust CIO and published by Pen & Sword between 2023 and 2025. It is necessary, though, to appreciate some key points. Firstly, the Battle of Britain was essentially a contest for aerial supremacy over southern England, from the Germans' perspective to facilitate a seaborne invasion of Britain. The battle is officially deemed to have begun on 10 July 1940, by which time Dowding's strength was twenty-five operational Hurricane squadrons and nineteen of Spitfires. Not all of these machines were deployed in southern England, however, as Dowding had to both maintain a substantial reserve in anticipation of heavy raids on the industrial north. By 16 August 1940, CS airscrews had been fitted to all Spitfires and Hurricanes, and, more importantly, on 22 August 1940, 611 Squadron received the first Spitfire Mk IIA. This improved Spitfire had a top speed of 370 mph, nearly 50 mph faster than the Hurricane and 15 mph more than the Me 109E. The Mk IIs rate of climb was 2,600 feet per minute – 473 feet more than the Mk IA. On 4 September 1940 the new Hurricane Mk II was delivered, with a top speed of 342 mph – 28 mph slower than the new Me 109E-4. Of absolutely crucial importance, however, is that the Spitfire Mk IIA's service ceiling was increased to 37,600 feet – 1,600 feet higher than the 109. It was simply impossible to improve the Hurricane significantly further, especially to make it a high-altitude fighter, which it was never going to be. As we have seen, in fighter combat height, sun and surprise are everything. Frequently the Me 109s came in very high, just below the stratosphere, and at heights in excess of 32,000 feet. Only the Spitfire Mk IIA could meet them at such heights, either on equal or advantageous terms. This is the most significant development in the Spitfire story thus far.

On 17 September 1940, realising that the *Luftwaffe* was unable to defeat Fighter Command, Hitler postponed his proposed invasion. By 30 September 1940, so heavy were German bomber casualties that the assault on Britain switched to night attacks. Indeed, the last major daylight raid on Britain occurred on 7 October 1940, and five days later Hitler cancelled the invasion indefinitely. So far as the Air Ministry was concerned, the Battle of Britain ended on 31 October 1940 in a British victory, although, uniquely, neither air force was defeated in the usual sense: Fighter Command remained an effective force with aerial superiority over its homeland, and the *Luftwaffe*, was still a force to be reckoned with and by night reducing various British cities to rubble. The fact remains, though, that the Germans failed to wrest aerial supremacy from Fighter Command to facilitate a seaborne invasion – and that was indeed a victory for Britain. By remaining in the war, Britain was ultimately able to become a base from which, with essential American aid, the Allied liberation of Europe could eventually be launched in 1944. The Spitfires and Hurricanes of Fighter Command, therefore, cost Hitler dearly in 1940.

By the spring of 1941, following a change of leadership, Fighter Command underwent a reorganisation, all sector stations accommodating a 'wing' of three squadrons; Hurricanes remained on the frontline at this time, but were in the process of being completely replaced by the superior Spitfire Mk II, the Spitfire's superior performance and potential for further development having been fully recognised. Adopting an offensive strategy, Fighter Command was now to 'reach out' and 'lean into France', taking the war to the Germans across the Channel. By this time, the Spitfire Mk IIB had a pair of cannon and four machine guns. Each cannon, however, weighed 96 lbs, excluding ammunition, so, the Mk II's Merlin XII engine was not powerful

PROLOGUE

enough to cope with this extra weight, leading to development of the Merlin 45 and introduction of the Spitfire Mk V. This new fighter had a top speed of 359 mph at 25,000 feet, which altitude it reached in eight minutes, and could achieve a maximum ceiling of 35,000 feet. By May 1941, the Spitfire Mk V was reaching the fighter squadrons in numbers.

Going forward into 1941's 'Non-stop Offensive', Fighter Command employed various types of aggressive operations, including so-called 'Rhubarbs', entailing pairs of Spitfires streaking low across the Channel to avoid radar detection and attacking targets of opportunity; 'Ramrods', which were similar but involving more aircraft and delivered against a specific target; strong fighter sweeps and more complex 'Circus' operations. In the latter, a small number of medium bombers were tasked with attacking targets in northern France and escorted by hundreds of Spitfires. Although such a small force of bombers was never going to inflict significant damage, their inclusion meant that the enemy could not ignore these incursions, the intention being that the massed RAF fighter formations would then destroy the German fighters piecemeal. Unfortunately, the record shows, however, that this was not the case. As there were no targets in occupied France of great strategic importance to the Germans, the *Luftwaffe* could choose carefully when to engage. Wisely, the Germans only attacked when the tactical situation was favourable to them. Furthermore, in what was an arms race, to the *Luftwaffe* now had the much-improved Me 109F, an altogether more curvaceous and elliptical design than the old *Emil*, and which was a match for the Spitfire Mk V. Taking advantage of their aircraft's technical strengths, the enemy pilots climbed very high, ambushing RAF formations from up-sun in fast passes. Given the benefits of fuel injection, the Germans' standard evasive tactic was to dive at full boost, this manoeuvre producing a stream of black smoke from the exhaust ports, leading many an RAF pilot to believe that his target had been hit and destroyed. In reality, the enemy machine would frequently pull up either in or below cloud, undamaged. We know now that the more fighters are engaged the greater will be the over-claiming factor, due to the speed and confusion involved, and as the RAF was fighting at high altitude, often above cloud, over France, intelligence officers had no wrecks to visit on the ground to verify. Fighter Command's claims during 1941, therefore, were unavoidably hugely inflated – providing a completely false impression of the 'Non-Stop Offensive's' progress. Throughout this time of cross-Channel operations, many experienced fighter leaders were lost: by the end of the 'season', Fighter Command was losing the battle by a ratio of over 2:1.

On 22 June 1941 Hitler invaded the Soviet Union, after which Britain came under increasing pressure from Stalin to provide aid and, in particular, open a second front. Given the complexities involved and resources required, with America still neutral, a landing in France was impossible. The only practical way of demonstrating support and was by continuing with the aerial campaign over northern France by day and Germany by night, the objective being to tie down *Luftwaffe* units on the Channel coast, thus relieving the pressure on the Russian front. This never happened. After the Battle of Britain German fighter units dispersed to other theatres, leaving just JG 26 and JG 2 on the Channel coast. These experienced and skilfully led units literally held the fort, and no German reinforcements were required. Then, in September 1941, a new menace appeared in dangerous French skies: the *Focke-Wulf* (FW) 190. The performance of this enemy machine was phenomenal. The aircraft's fourteen cylinder, 1,700 hp, BMW radial engine provided a maximum speed of 312 mph at 15,000 feet; with a one-minute override boost it could exceed 400 mph. With a maximum service ceiling of 35,000 feet, the 190 could reach 26,000 feet – the height around which most combats were commonly fought – in twelve minutes, and was extremely manoeuvrable. By comparison, the Spitfire Mk V's maximum speed at 20,000 feet was 371 mph. It was unable to operate efficiently above 25,000 feet, by which altitude the top speed had dropped to 359 mph and took fifteen minutes top reach. Significantly, for the first time, an enemy fighter could out-turn the Spitfire.

As RAF losses mounted, for the first time Spitfire pilots lost confidence in their aircraft, their radius of penetration being restricted to the French coast. 1941 was not a good year for Fighter Command, but on the world stage the balance of power had shifted: on 7 December 1941, Japan made a surprise attack on the American Pacific Fleet at Pearl Harbor. With America now in the war at last, and Hitler fighting on two fronts, Britain's reward for having

PROLOGUE

remained free and continuing war against Germany, although still far off, was nonetheless in sight.

Naturally, given the FW 190 threat, there was great pressure for Spitfire performance to be increased. The answer was the Spitfire Mk IX, which was essentially a Mk V airframe, the nose of which was slightly extended to accommodate the new Merlin 61 engine. With a top speed of 409 mph at 28,000 feet, maximum service ceiling of 43,000 feet, and a climbing speed of 4,000 feet per minute, this was the fighter that Fighter Command so desperately needed. In July 1942, comparison trials were undertaken between a Spitfire Mk IX and a recently captured FW 190, the result favouring the new Spitfire, with which Fighter Command began re-equipping the following month. On 30 July 1942, the Mk IX achieved its first success over the FW 190, and, on 12 September 1942 destroyed an enemy high-altitude reconnaissance bomber at an incredible 43,000 feet. Suddenly, morale was restored, and RAF pilots were once again able to wage war on a fair footing. Indeed, the Spitfire Mk IX became the most numerous of all 24 Spitfire marks, with a total of 5,710 being built.

The Spitfire, however, had been designed as a short-range defensive interceptor. It was not created to fulfil the role of a cross-Channel offensive fighter or bomber escort. The operations of 1941, however, had seen the Spitfire pilots doing both these things. By the spring of 1942, the United States Eighth Air Force was operating from bases in England, determined to perfect accurate daylight bombing of targets in Germany itself. The problem was that the Spitfire Mk IX's range, even with a 30-gallon auxiliary fuel tank, was only 980 miles. This meant that the American bombers could only be escorted so far over enemy occupied territory before the escorting fighters had to turn back, re-fuel and meet their charges when homeward bound. Of course, the period of time when the bomber formations were unprotected was when the enemy fighters struck. From this point onwards, the lack of a long-range fighter became of increasing concern to the Allies – a role later fulfilled by American fighters such as the P-51 Mustang, P-38 Lightning and P-47 Thunderbolt.

Control of the Mediterranean was also bitterly contested during the first half of the war. Geographically, the key to that theatre was the tiny island of

Malta, on the supply route to North Africa where British forces were engaged with those of Germany and Italy. For three weeks in 1940, in fact, the island's defence was undertaken by three antiquated Gladiator biplanes, known as 'Faith', 'Hope' and 'Charity'. At the end of June 1941, four Hurricanes arrived and throughout the following month these 7 fighters resisted the best efforts of some 200 enemy aircraft based in Sicily. So furiously did the defenders fight, in fact, that eventually the Italians, like the Germans over England, were forced to operate only at night. More Hurricanes arrived but by March 1942 the Italians had been joined by superior *Luftwaffe* units and the contest was at its height. That month, fifteen Spitfires flew off the aircraft carrier HMS *Eagle*, landing at Takali: within three days the Spitfires had destroyed their first enemy aircraft. In an effort to destroy the Spitfire force, Takali was bombed repeatedly: by 2 April 1942, not one complete section of Spitfires remained operational. Indeed, the defenders thought themselves lucky if they could field six fighters at any one time: two for airfield defence and four to intercept.

On 15 April 1942, Malta was awarded the George Cross, and five days later forty-seven more Spitfires reach the besieged island. Following further intense attacks, a day later only eighteen Spitfires were serviceable; two days on, none were airworthy. For some unknown reason, though, the *Luftwaffe* eased off the pressure, enabling sixty-four Spitfires, flying off the aircraft carriers USS *Wasp* and HMS *Eagle*, to get through to Malta. A clever system was devised to rapidly turn the aircraft around, to prevent them being caught on the ground: six Spitfires were up again within just six minutes of landing! By 23 October 1942, the Germans had been defeated in the Western Desert, and soon, after the Americans landed, the Allies were rolling up North Africa from both directions. The defence of Malta has rightly become legendary, but Spitfire operations from the island are important for another reason: it was from Malta that Spitfire fighter bombers first flew, two 500 lb bombs carried beneath their wings, attacking enemy airfields in Sicily. This was yet another role not envisaged by the Spitfire's designer, indicating the airframe's strength and versatility. Spitfires had also flown in the Desert Air Force during the North African campaign, and many of these units now gathered on Malta ready for the push into Europe via Sicily. From Malta the

PROLOGUE

Spitfire wings swept over Sicily in an attempt to bring German fighters to battle, in much the same way as was happening over northern France.

By now, P-51 Mustangs, with a range of 2,200 miles, were fulfilling a dedicated escort role from English airfields, as the American daylight bomber offensive continued, slowly relieving the Spitfire of this role. As ever, the war's progress dictated Spitfire deployment: 1941 and 1942 had been disastrous years for the Allies in the Far East, culminating in the Fall of Singapore on 15 February 1942 – Britain's greatest military defeat. With a full-scale British retreat from Burma underway, it seemed that the Japanese were unstoppable, Japan's control of New Guinea putting the Australian mainland within range of their bombers. Three squadrons of Spitfires, however, were based near Darwin: on 2 May 1942, thirty-three Spitfire Mk Vs successfully engaged the first major Japanese raid on Darwin. The Spitfire was faster than the Japanese Mitsubushi Zero fighter, and the light enemy machine was vulnerable to cannon fire. With the Americans sending an increasing amount of troops to the Pacific theatre, beginning their 'Island Hopping' campaign, pressure began mounting on the so-far victorious Japanese, the Spitfire again playing its part.

Over enemy occupied Europe, the Spitfire's war continued largely unchanged. On 24 February 1943 the Spitfire Mk XII reached the RAF, heralding a new phase of Spitfire development. This machine looked very different from the early Merlin-engined variants, largely because it had a completely new Rolls-Royce Griffon engine, and was an interim expedient, pending arrival of the improved Mk XIV. Intended for low-altitude sorties, the Mk XII's top speed was 397 mph. By October, the Mk XIV was in service, with a maximum speed of 448 mph, a service ceiling of 45,500 feet. Impressive though these statistics were, the fact remained that the new Spitfire's range was only 850 miles.

On 9 July 1943, Spitfires supported the Allied invasion of Sicily. It was really from hereon that the air war, and the Spitfire's role within it, began changing significantly, the advancing Allied armies need for close air support meaning that the Spitfire increasingly became a fighter bomber, not so much mixing it with the *Luftwaffe* but dive bombing and strafing German strongpoints and troops. On 3 September 1943, the Allies spring boarded from Sicily to invade Italy, landing at Salerno, and joining Spitfires in providing air cover were Supermarine Seafires, the carrier version of this famous fighters.

Having undertaken major combined operations and harnessed tactical air power in the Western Desert, Sicily and Italy, the Allies next planned to launch the liberation of enemy occupied Europe from British soil. To effect the necessary air operations in advance of and after the proposed landings, the Second Tactical Air Force (TAF) was created. In August 1943, the fighter wings based at the various sector stations became known as 'airfields'. These formations began practising living a nomadic existence, living under canvas and being self-sufficient, able to move quickly and at short notice, keeping up with the advancing army. By now, the *Luftwaffe* was seriously under pressure, defending the *Reich* by day against American bombers and RAF Bomber Command's 'heavies' at night. Moreover, after the catastrophic German defeat at Stalingrad in February 1943, Stalin's forces were advancing ever westwards. In the Far East too, the tide had long since turned, and the Allies were advancing on all fronts – albeit at great cost. Clearly the time was fast approaching for a cataclysmic finale – in which the Spitfire would continue to play its part.

Throughout 1943 and 1944, American military personnel and matériel had stock-piled in England ready for the long awaited second front. Such a huge, combined operation was unprecedented: the complex plan called for airborne troops to alight in Normandy in advance of the main landings, capturing key objectives; a huge aerial and naval bombardment would then soften coastal defences before Allied troops and armour landed on the beaches of Normandy. This Allied invasion – D-Day – the greatest combined operation in history, famously went ahead on 6 June 1944, a huge screen of fighters ensuring that the *Luftwaffe* failed to hinder the landings. Before and after D-Day, however, Spitfires continued to be employed as fighter bombers, harassing and destroying the enemy wherever he could be found. So complete, in fact, was Allied air superiority over the Normandy battlefield that the Germans were only able to move troops under cover of darkness. Soon, Spitfires were operating from French soil, extending their range of penetration over enemy territory. By mid-August 1944, the Germans had

PROLOGUE

no choice but to retreat across the river Seine via what became known as the 'Falaise Gap'. There the Allied fighter bombers pounded the enemy – German casualties are estimated at some 300,000; only 20,000 German soldiers safely crossed the Seine.

The following month, the ambitious but ill-fated Operation Market Garden was launched by Allied airborne forces, aimed at capture bridges across key rivers in the Netherlands, enabling the Allies to by-pass the Siegfried Line and enter Germany 'through the back door'. Whereas the American airborne forces successfully captured all of their objectives, British and Polish forces suffered a heavy defeat in Arnhem – the fabled 'bridge too far' – a combination of bad weather and close fighting making air support impossible. Consequently, the operation was only partially successful, the Allies not crossing the Rhine until 23 March 1945, beginning the 'long trek' into Germany.

During mid-1944, a new German fighter had been committed to battle – the jet-powered Me 262. With a top speed of 559 mph, the 262's debut heralded the end of all piston-engined fighters. The 262 represented the first of a whole new generation of aircraft, the performance of which was incomparable to the existing types in service. Nonetheless, on 5 October 1944 the Spitfires of 401 (RCAF) Squadron caught and destroyed the first enemy jet to be despatched: invincible the 262 may not have been, but its superior performance and the jet engine's potential for future development was clear to all. Not the 262 or Hitler's rocket bombs, the V-1 and V-2, however, could turn the tide of war, which had long been lost for Nazi Germany. With Allied and Soviet troops having linked up on the Elbe, as the Battle for Berlin raged in the doomed city, and the *Reich* lay in ruins all around, Hitler committed suicide on 30 April 1945. On 8 May 1945, Germany surrendered unconditionally, concluding the war in Europe.

The war in the Fast East, however, had yet to end. Hurricanes had equipped the RAF air component operating in that theatre until the arrival of Spitfires and P-51s in 1944. In spite of the long-term sea blockade and fire-bombing of Japanese cities, this Far Eastern adversary continued to fight determinedly. By July 1945, the carriers of Task Force 37 were in the Pacific, just 30 miles from Tokyo. Terminally weakened by the blockade, however,

Japan surrendered unconditionally, on 15 August 1945, after the second of two atomic bombs was dropped by the Americans. The Second World War was over at last.

The Supermarine Spitfire had entered the Second World War as the RAF's best front-line fighter. By 1945, the RAF had one squadron equipped with a jet fighter, the Gloster Meteor, which was the shape of things to come. Throughout the war, Spitfire had gone through so many modifications and improvements that the Griffon-engined growlers of 1944 onwards bore little resemblance to the little Merlin-engined prototype that first flew from Eastleigh in 1936. The Spitfire was originally envisaged and designed as a short-range defensive interceptor, a role in which it excelled, and had been pressed into service as a long-range offensive and escort fighter, high altitude interceptor and photographic reconnaissance machine, low-level fighter bomber and, known as the Seafire, even operated from aircraft carriers; it had flown and fought on all fronts, and was also operated by foreign powers, including both America and Russia. All of this provides ample evidence of the flexibility and long-term potential of Mitchell's design: that the Spitfire was ahead of its time in 1936 is indisputable, and this iconic aircraft occupies a unique place in history, hearts and minds.

The majority of photographs that follow originate in the personal albums of those who built, flew, and maintained Spitfires – the Spitfire story belongs to them, and in these largely unofficial snapshots we are able to peer through a misty window and get a very real idea of the Spitfire at war…

Spitfire
The Photographic Kaleidoscope

The brilliant British aircraft designer R.J. Mitchell, chief designer at Supermarine. His advanced thinking regarding the superiority of monoplanes led to the Spitfire. Sadly, Mitchell died prematurely, aged 42, on 11 June 1937 – his work on a heavy bomber design unfinished.

SPITFIRE: THE ICONIC FIGHTER IN UNIQUE PHOTOGRAPHS

Mitchell's Schneider Trophy winning S6 seaplane racer. The sleek lines are clearly apparent.

The only known photograph of R.J. Mitchell with his prototype Spitfire, K5054, photographed at Eastleigh by his son, Gordon.

Prototype Spitfire K5054.

SPITFIRE

The Supermarine factory before the war, situated on the banks of the river Itchen at Southampton. The site no longer exists, having been cleared in more recent times to make way for the Itchen Bridge.

Early Spitfire fuselages under construction at Supermarine.

SPITFIRE: THE ICONIC FIGHTER IN UNIQUE PHOTOGRAPHS

Left: Supermarine test pilot Jeffrey Quill over the Supermarine works in K5054 – now resplendent in war paint.

Below: Naturally Supermarine fanfared their new fighter. This is the cover of the original promotional catalogue, *circa* 1938.

SPITFIRE

Spitfire evolution – from Schneider Trophy racer to 'real killer fighter'.

SPITFIRE: THE ICONIC FIGHTER IN UNIQUE PHOTOGRAPHS

The Spitfire was first delivered to Duxford's 19 Squadron on 4 August 1938. Here, the squadron's Spitfire Mk Is are lined up for the press in 1939. Note the fixed pitch propeller, lack of armoured glass, un-faired radio mast and pre-war 'WZ' codes.

A close-up of a 19 Squadron Spitfire Mk I.

A close-up indicating the thin wing section and Browning machine-gun ports.

No. 19 Squadron Mk Is in flight.

SPITFIRE: THE ICONIC FIGHTER IN UNIQUE PHOTOGRAPHS

Given developments in Germany, the Spitfire was soon fitted with the de Havilland two-pitch, three-bladed airscrew. This factory-fresh machine is one of those aircraft, designated Mk IA. By now the Spitfire's windscreen was armoured, the sliding canopy blown, improving visibility, and the radio mast faired.

One of 19 Squadron's original Mk Is at Duxford in September 1939. Although the aircraft's propeller, windscreen and canopy has been updated, the un-faired radio mast remains. This was the personal aircraft of Flight Lieutenant Brian Lane, commander of 'A' Flight, who always flew letter 'K'. Note also the new Squadron code of 'QV'.

Flight Lieutenant Lane in that same Spitfire Mk IA. Note the armoured windscreen, reflector gunsight, pilot's headrest and emergency punch-out panel in the sliding Perspex canopy. The artwork on the cockpit door is also interesting, showing a swastika shattered by a lightning bolt; all of Lane's Spitfires were called '*Blitzen*'.

Another 19 Squadron Mk IA in the early war camouflage scheme featuring a half white and half black under surface. In the foreground is the Alsatian 'Flash' belonging to Flight Sergeant George 'Grumpy' Unwin, posing as a fighter pilot!

SPITFIRE: THE ICONIC FIGHTER IN UNIQUE PHOTOGRAPHS

Above left: A close-up of the same aircraft.

Above right: Flight Sergeant Unwin's leather flying helmet, goggles and canvas oxygen/radio mask positioned on his Spitfire's wingtip, ready for take-off. Note the wing tip landing light. Unwin was the first NCO pilot to fly a Spitfire – later becoming one of Fighter Command's most aggressive pilots in the Battle of Britain.

No. 19 Squadron's first Spitfire flying accident. Two aircraft, K9854, flown by Pilot Officer Eric Ball, and this, K9821, flown by Flying Officer Wilf Clouston, collided mid-air. Clouston forced-landed on Newmarket racecourse – fortunately both pilots were unhurt.

SPITFIRE

Flight Lieutenant Brian Lane leading 19 Squadron's 'A' Flight over Cambridgeshire in early 1940. This rare air-to-air snapshot was taken by Pilot Officer Michael Lyne.

A Spitfire Mk IA of 66 Squadron airborne from Duxford in early 1940.

SPITFIRE: THE ICONIC FIGHTER IN UNIQUE PHOTOGRAPHS

Left: To increase the numbers of operational squadrons available, the Auxiliary Air Force (AAF) was formed before the war. This is Pilot Officer Denis Adams of the AAF's Spitfire-equipped 611 Squadron 'West Lancashire' Squadron early in 1940. The aircraft is an early Mk IA, still lacking a rear-view mirror. Note the tented accommodation in the background.

Below, opposite above and opposite below: Another AAF unit was 616 'South Yorkshire' Squadron, the Spitfire Mk IAs of which are seen here at Leconfield during early 1940.

SPITFIRE

SPITFIRE: THE ICONIC FIGHTER IN UNIQUE PHOTOGRAPHS

In March 1940, Pilot Officer 'Teddy' St Aubyn pranged a 616 Squadron Spitfire at Leconfield whilst landing at night.

A 'vic' of 602 Squadron Spitfire Mk IAs over flies another squadron machine at Drem, early 1940. The wheeled devices are accumulator battery trollies, plugged into the aircraft to start the Merlin engine.

A factory-fresh Spitfire Mk IA, bearing the code letters of 609 'West Riding' Squadron, another AAF unit, about to undertake a test flight at Eastleigh, Southampton in 1940. It was there that final assembly and testing took place.

The same Spitfire being pushed into position for take-off by the groundcrew. Typically, this comprised an engine fitter, airframe and instrument fitter, and armourers.

SPITFIRE: THE ICONIC FIGHTER IN UNIQUE PHOTOGRAPHS

No. 609 Squadron's Pilot Officer David Crook about to taxi for take-off from Northolt during Operation Dynamo, the air operation covering the Dunkirk evacuation in May 1940. It was over the French coast that the Spitfire met the Me 109 for the first time – and, in spite of poor tactical formations, acquitted itself well.

A Section of 64 Squadron Spitfires scramble from Kenley during the Battle of Britain.

SPITFIRE

A flight of 610 'County of Chester' Squadron's Spitfires demonstrate the tight 'vic' formation prescribed by Fighter Command – but which proved disastrous in combat.

A Spitfire of 64 Squadron, flaps down, lands at Kenley during the Battle of Britain.

The same aircraft taxies in. Note the rear-view mirror, in this case faired into the windscreen.

Spitfires being re-armed – a still from an RAF training film.

No. 609 Squadron's Pilot Officer David Crook ready for take-off, Warmwell, August 1940.

Crook's Spitfire being rapidly 'turned around' between combats on *Adlertag*, 13 August 1940.

Spitfire K9894 of 234 Squadron, in which Pilot Officer Derek Robinson was shot down by Me 109s on 8 August 1940 – the pilot survived the wheels-up crash-landing.

Personal photography on service installations was prohibited, but a surprising number of snapshots were taken by proud airman posing with their aircraft. This dawn photograph was taken at Kirton-in-Lindsey of 222 Squadron's Spitfire Mk IA P9318 and Pilot Officer Laurie Whitbread by Sergeant Reg Johnson.

Pilot Officer Whitbread then returned the favour, photographing Sergeant Johnson beside the same Spitfire. Interestingly, the rear-view mirror is housed within the windscreen assembly.

SPITFIRE: THE ICONIC FIGHTER IN UNIQUE PHOTOGRAPHS

No. 222 Squadron was heavily engaged flying from Hornchurch during the Battle of Britain. Like 11 Group's other sector stations it was heavily bombed – this is one of the squadron's wrecked Spitfires after a particularly heavy raid on 31 August 1940.

Above: Spitfires of 222 and 603 Squadrons at Hornchurch in early September 1940. 'XT-M' is the aircraft in which Pilot Officer Richard Hillary, author of *The Last Enemy*, was shot down in flames on 3 September 1940. Note the steamroller repairing bomb damage.

Opposite above: 222 Squadron fitter Joe Crowshaw sat in Spitfire P9323. This aircraft was shot down over the Isle of Sheppey on 31 August 1940.

Opposite below: Flight Lieutenant Gillies prepares for a sortie from Gravesend, a Hurricane of 501 Squadron in the background. Sadly Gillies was killed in action on 4 October 1940. (*via Ron Smith*)

SPITFIRE

A pilot of 74 Squadron at Hornchurch, the photograph showing the 'trolly acc' plugged in.

In June 1940, 19 Squadron received experimental Spitfire Mk IBs, armed with two 20-mm cannons. Unfortunately, due to jamming, the type was unsuccessful and withdrawn in September 1940. This is the only photograph of one such Spitfire known to exist, and was taken at Fowlmere by Squadron Leader Brian Lane.

No. 19 Squadron's Mk IBs were replaced by machine-gun armed Mk IAs. Here Sergeant Jennings overflies another squadron aircraft at Fowlmere in September 1940.

Sergeant Jennings prepares to scramble for the camera, his engine already running.

Sergeant Jennings takes off from Fowlmere in QV-I, X4474.

Sergeant Jennings and Spitfire Mk IA X4474: both are pictured in their natural environment.

SPITFIRE: THE ICONIC FIGHTER IN UNIQUE PHOTOGRAPHS

Another posed photograph: back at Fowlmere, armourer Fred Roberts re-arms Sergeant Jennings's Spitfire.

A 19 Squadron Spitfire is turned around for real at Fowlmere, September 1940.

No. 616 Squadron also operated from Fowlmere in September 1940, whilst participating in 12 Group Wing operations. Here one of that squadron's Mk IAs prepares for flight. Note the 'chocks' in place.

The Mk Spitfire IA of 19 Squadron's CO, Squadron Leader Brian Lane. Of interest is the unusual outsize fuselage roundel and yellow propeller spinner. This machine ultimately perished with its pilot in a Scottish flying accident.

SPITFIRE: THE ICONIC FIGHTER IN UNIQUE PHOTOGRAPHS

On 5 September 1940, 19 Squadron's Pilot Officer Eric Burgoyne was attacked by an Me 109 over Hornchurch: this is the result of being hit by 20-mm cannon fire. It is often said that the Hurricane could absorb great damage and keep flying – the photographic evidence suggests that, contrary to popular belief, so could the Spitfire. Interestingly this aircraft's individual serial number, P9391, appears painted across the tail top, rather than on the usual after fuselage.

Pilot Officer Bob Beardsley of 41 Squadron at Hornchurch, whose Spitfire Mk IA shows to good effect the armoured windscreen, reflector gunsight and externally mounted rear-view mirror.

Sergeant Terry Healey of 41 Squadron confers with his armourers at Hornchurch.

Sergeant Terry Healey of 41 Squadron with his Spitfire at Hornchurch – victory tallies have been chalked on the cockpit side – including two RAF roundels and a question mark! Identity of the 'photo bomber' raising the 'two fingered salute' is unknown!

Spitfire Mk IA K9894 of 152 Squadron, in which Sergeant Denis Robinson was shot down in combat with Me 109s of II/JG 53 off Swanage on 8 August 1940 – the pilot survived the crash-landing.

SPITFIRE

A Spitfire Mk IA of 602 Squadron at Westhampnett (now Goodwood), a Tangmere satellite airfield in 1940 – the red doped canvas patches protecting the gun ports from debris during take-off and landing are visible, and the wing leading edge wavy camouflage demarcation line is untypical.

A 234 Squadron Spitfire having crash-landed at St Eval during the 'Spitfire Summer' of 1940.

A Spitfire of 234 Squadron returns safely to St Eval during the Battle of Britain.

A 602 Squadron Spitfire Mk IA at Drem, early 1940.

SPITFIRE

On 6 September 1940, *Hauptmann* Hubertus von Bonin of I/JG 54 damaged a Spitfire over the Channel, the pilot of which, Pilot Officer James Caistor, forced-landed near Calais, where he was captured; his aircraft, X4260, was put back in the air and evaluated by the Germans.

The small factory of Vickers-Supermarine at Woolston was unable to cope with producing sufficient Spitfires. Consequently Lord Nuffield was charged with overseeing the opening of a new Spitfire plant at Castle Bromwich, which applied the mass-production methods of the automotive industry to making Spitfires.

Above and below: Another view of Spitfires being made at Castle Bromwich. Surprisingly, the *Luftwaffe* never mounted a major raid against this crucial target.

After the Supermarine factory at Woolston was devastated by the raids of September 1940, Spitfire production was widely dispersed to various workshop premises, temporary and otherwise, around Hampshire and Wiltshire. The Castle Bromwich Aeroplane Factory also adopted this process: these women are producing wing leading edges at the premises of Rackstraw's cabinet makers in Worcester. The completed items were sent to Castle Bromwich and absorbed into the final assembly process.

The first Spitfires produced at Castle Bromwich were the new Mk IIAs, which reached the squadrons during the Battle of Britain. An improvement over the previous two-pitch propeller was the Dowty Rotol Constant Speed Airscrew, seen here with its broader blades, made of laminated wood covered in a plastic-like material called Jablo. This example, of 19 Squadron, was snapped at Fowlmere with Czech pilot František Hradil – he was later shot down and killed over Southend.

Above: Squadron Leader Lane's Mk IIA at Fowlmere, displaying his rank pennant. This machine was fitted not only with the common external rear-view mirror but also with locally improvised side-mounted mirrors.

Left: A phenomenon in 1940 was the spontaneous expression of support for Fighter Command that manifested itself in the so-called 'Spitfire Funds'. Promotional posters such as this were commonplace and supporting the local fund became seen as a patriotic duty. It also provided a means for the Home Front to hit back against the enemy bombers, by buying Spitfires for the government.

SPITFIRE

The cash generated by Spitfire Funds did not, in reality, have any effect on Spitfire production, but nonetheless served a valuable purpose by getting the Home Front involved. The activity peaked during the Battle of Britain, and by early 1941 Spitfires with serial numbers designated as being 'presentation' aircraft were beginning to appear. The donor's name was applied to the fuselage in yellow paint at the factory, where the machines were photographed for publicity purposes. This is a Mk IIA, P8045, 'City of Worcester I', built at Castle Bromwich in February 1941.

Senior Canadian officers at the handover ceremony of Spitfire Mk IIA, P8044, 'First Canadian Division' to 41 Squadron at Catterick in early 1941.

SPITFIRE: THE ICONIC FIGHTER IN UNIQUE PHOTOGRAPHS

Pilot Officer Peter Brown of 41 Squadron aloft in P8044.

No. 66 Squadron flew from Exeter in early 1941, one of the Squadron's Mk IIs seen here being maintained on trestles. This is P7843, 'Aldergrove', presented by *The Belfast Telegraph* Spitfire Fund.

This presentation Spitfire began life as a Mk IA, before being upgraded to Mk V status. R7195, 'Holmewood', was one of four aircraft presented by the High Sheriff of Cambridge. This machine had a long service life, during which Pilot Officer Phil Archer of 92 Squadron at Biggin Hill – where this photograph was taken – destroyed two Me 109s in June and July 1941. During the latter combat 'Holmewood' was damaged and Archer was wounded. It was eventually lost on a weather reconnaissance flight over Le Touquet in 1944. Protruding from the wing blister is the mechanism used to load the 20-mm ammunition drum.

In addition to individual aircraft, there were also presentation squadrons: these are Spitfire Mk VBs of 91 'Nigeria' Squadron at Hawkinge in 1942.

SPITFIRE: THE ICONIC FIGHTER IN UNIQUE PHOTOGRAPHS

Amongst the first wing leaders appointed in March 1941, was the legless Wing Commander Douglas Bader DSO DFC, who chose Tangmere, near Chichester. This is Mk IIA P7966, 'Manxman', bearing the Wing Leader's initials, 'DB'.

Bader, arguably, rightly or wrongly, the most famous Spitfire pilot of all time, exiting P7966 at Westhampnett after an offensive sortie during the summer of 1941; the 'Wingco' appears to be wearing a German kapok-filled life jacket.

SPITFIRE

Above: Spitfire 'Dogsbody' was the first to be fitted with a colour cine-gun camera, made by Kodak, which was installed in the field at Westhampnett during the early summer of 1941. Of great interest is the wing leader's nose-art: Hitler being kicked in the backside by a flying boot, similar to the artwork applied to Bader's 242 Squadron Hurricane during the Battle of Britain.

Right: The camera installed in P7966.

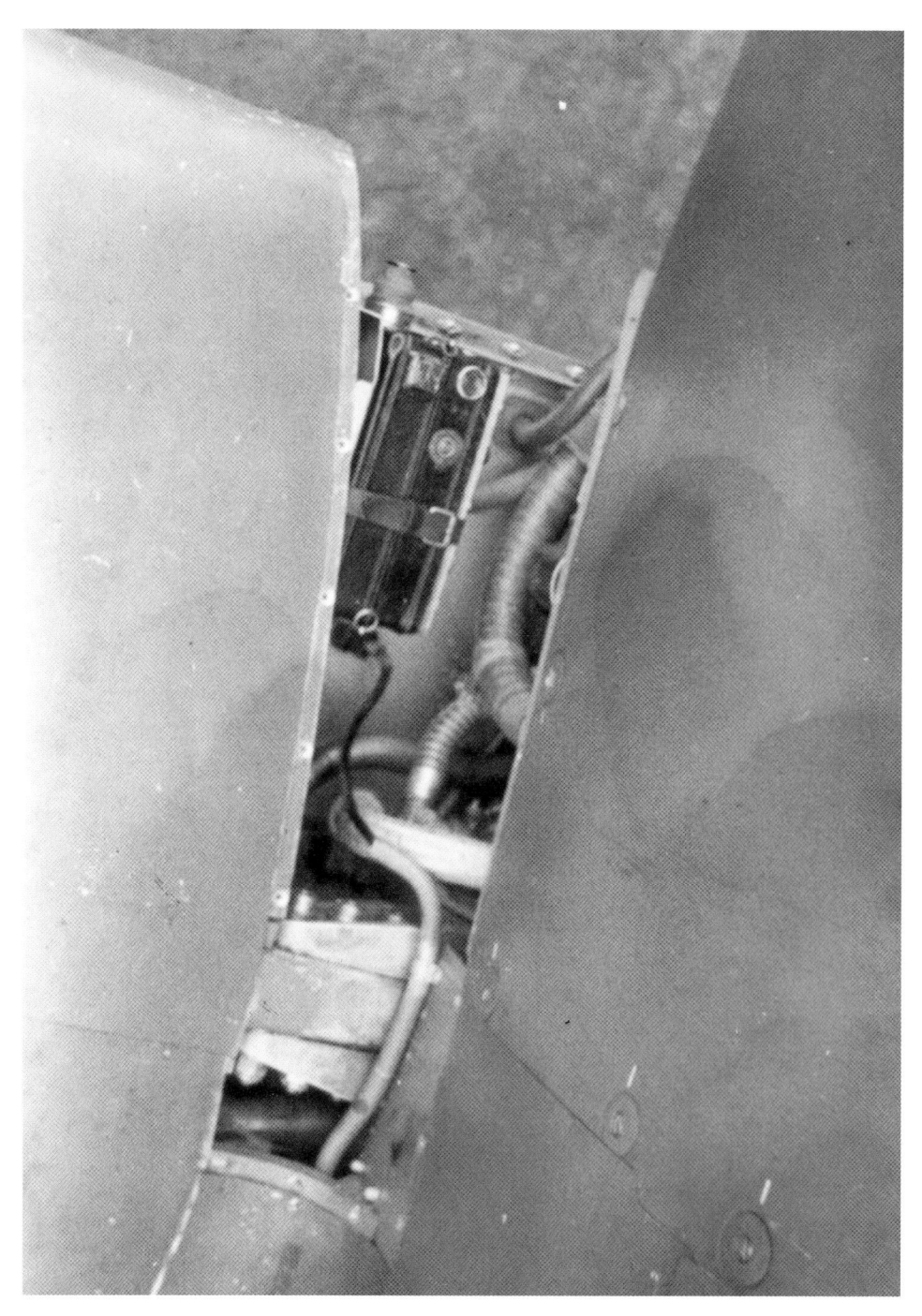

A Spitfire cine-gun camera installation (in a different aircraft) viewed from above. These were of great value to intelligence officers in analysing aerial combats.

Spitfire Mk IIA, P7925, 'Weston-Super-Mare', was another presentation Spitfire produced by Castle Bromwich in February 1941 – the aircraft was finally struck off charge in 1947.

In 1940, the Sutton-in-Ashfield Spitfire Fund raised £5,126 in just eight weeks, funding this machine, Mk IA R7193, 'The Snipe', which went to Canada for photographic reconnaissance trials.

SPITFIRE: THE ICONIC FIGHTER IN UNIQUE PHOTOGRAPHS

In the winter of 1940/1941, various Mk II airframes were upgraded to Mk V specification, this example being P8714, 'Spirit of Warrington II' – which failed to return from operations on 15 October 1941.

The Southampton Spitfire Fund raised enough to present three Spitfires, amongst them, appropriately, 'R.J. Mitchell', R7058, which became an instructional airframe.

Throughout, the Spitfire was also a potent weapon in the propaganda war – a depiction seen here on a Royal Australian Air Force recruiting poster.

SPITFIRE: THE ICONIC FIGHTER IN UNIQUE PHOTOGRAPHS

The Battle of Britain officially ended on 31 October 1940, although the fighter forces of both sides clashed over southern England and the Channel until February 1941. By night, of course, the Germans rained down bombs upon British cities, not least Coventry. Fighter Command, however, prepared for the daylight battles of the 'season' ahead. Squadrons were rotated so that battle-weary units could rest, re-fit and train new pilots. No. 65 Squadron, for example, had been hotly engaged during the summer of 1940, but on 26 February 1941 flew north, to Kirton-in-Lindsey, exchanging its new Mk IIs with the old Mk IAs of 616 Squadron, which relieved the unit at Tangmere. This is Sergeant Johnson (right) of 65 Squadron pictured with one of those Mk IAs at Kirton-in-Lindsey, with an unknown Polish pilot. In fact, the aircraft has the Polish air force chequered red and white square insignia applied below the windscreen. The aircraft also has one wing under surface painted black, which was a camouflage scheme used between 27 November 1940 and 22 April 1941.

Pilot Officer Jack Strang, a New Zealander serving with 65 'East India' Squadron, seated in a Mk IA at Kirton-in-Lindsey during the winter of 1940. Unusually given this date, this machine still has an unfaired radio mast and no rear-view mirror whatsoever. Strang was later reported missing in action.

SPITFIRE: THE ICONIC FIGHTER IN UNIQUE PHOTOGRAPHS

A close-up of a 65 Squadron Mk IIA at Westhampnett in early 1941, the 'sky' band around the tail indicating it to be a day fighter.

Sergeant Hugh Chalmers of 65 Squadron exiting a Mk IIA at Tangmere in early 1941 – the de-icing system can be seen on the windscreen.

A pilot of 65 Squadron in his cumbersome parachute, and Spitfire IIA YT-T.

Sergeant Ron Stillwell about to go in 65 Squadron's YT-X – the fitter is cleaning the canopy: to see was to live longer.

SPITFIRE: THE ICONIC FIGHTER IN UNIQUE PHOTOGRAPHS

On 26 February 1941, 65 Squadron was relieved at Tangmere by 616 Squadron, the two units exchanging Spitfires: the former inherited 65's Mk IIAs, whilst the latter flew to Kirton-in-Lindsey in 616's tired Mk IAs. These are pilots of 65 Squadron thereafter with one of those Mk IAs – amongst them (third right) is the great ace Flying Officer Brendon 'Paddy' Finucane, later reported missing whilst leading the Kenley Wing.

Flying Officer Finucane (standing at left) and friends with another 65 Squadron Mk IA at Kirton-in-Lindsey.

The Belfast Telegraph was an enthusiastic promoter of the Spitfire Fund, ultimately presenting sixteen aircraft. This is another of them, P7849, which joined 19 Squadron at Fowlmere in March 1941. The pilot is Squadron Leader Walter Lawson DFC, later reported missing.

'Armagh' aloft, flown by Squadron Leader Lawson. The 'L' shaped device is the air speed indicator.

SPITFIRE: THE ICONIC FIGHTER IN UNIQUE PHOTOGRAPHS

Another unofficial 'Armagh' snapshot at Fowlmere in early 1941: Sergeant David Cox.

Pilot Officer Stevens at Fowlmere in 1941 with Spitfire Mk IIA 'Red Rose', P7920, one of four Spitfires presented by the Lancashire Constabulary and Wardens' Service; the aircraft was ultimately struck off charge following a landing accident in 1944.

Opposite: Spitfire Mk IIAs of 19 Squadron up from Fowlmere in early 1941.

SPITFIRE

SPITFIRE: THE ICONIC FIGHTER IN UNIQUE PHOTOGRAPHS

A section of 616 Squadron Spitfires up from Westhampnett, summer 1941 – bound for action over France.

Sergeant E.W. 'Peter' Merriman of the Tangmere Wing's 610 Squadron, summer 1941, with P8670, 'Second City of London Textile', ultimately struck off charge after being damaged in combat.

Sergeants Doley and Horner of 610 Squadron inspecting the damage suffered in a flying accident by Spitfire R6599 at Acklington.

Sergeant W.J. 'Johnny' Johnson of the Tangmere Wing's 145 Squadron aloft from Merston, summer 1941.

Flight Lieutenant Newling's 145 Squadron Spitfire Mk IIA.

No. 145 Squadron's Sergeant Frank Twitchett's 'War Horse', P7990.

SPITFIRE

Above: The crew of Frank Twitchett's Spitfire, Drew and Pattison.

Right: On 21 June 1941, Sergeant Twitchett had a lucky escape when attacked by a Me 109 over France in Spitfire P8341, returning to Merston with a badly damaged tail. According to popular myth, the sturdier looking Hurricane could absorb more damage than a Spitfire and still keep flying – but this is unsupported by the actual evidence, given countless examples of Spitfires also returning home when badly shot-up.

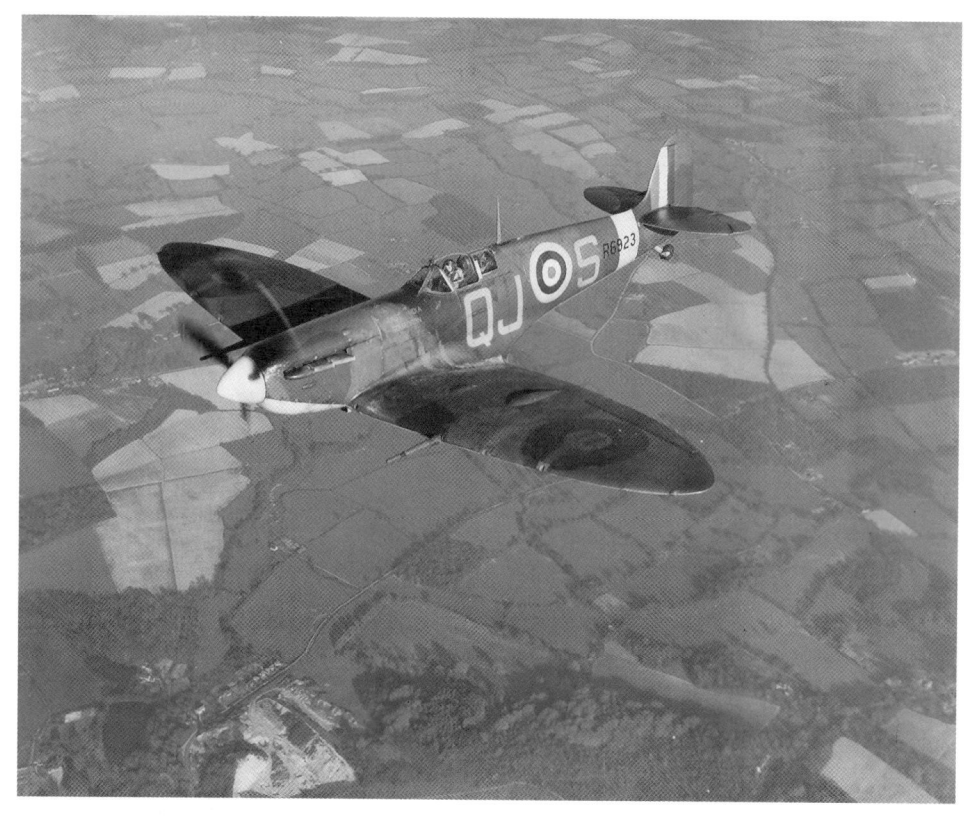

SPITFIRE: THE ICONIC FIGHTER IN UNIQUE PHOTOGRAPHS

Above and below: The Mk IIs, which included the cannon-armed IIB, were replaced by the improved Spitfire Mk V, the 'A' version armed with machine guns, the 'B' with two cannon and four machine guns. These are fine studies of Mk VBs, showing the cannon to good effect.

Opposite: Spitfire Mk VB AA879, 'Manchester Civil Defender' of 616 Squadron being re-armed at Kingscliffe.

SPITFIRE

A Spitfire Mk VB of 616 Squadron undergoing maintenance at Kingscliffe.

Pilot Officer Victor Lawson of 65 Squadron at Debden in a Spitfire Mk VB in 1942.

SPITFIRE

A Spitfire Mk VB of 72 Squadron having its guns harmonised at Biggin Hill.

The Spitfire Mk VB of 610 Squadron's Flight Lieutenant Denis Crowley-Milling, pictured at Ludham.

Flight Lieutenant Crowley-Milling's anonymous groundcrew.

Spitfire down: The crash site of Flight Lieutenant L.H. 'Buck' Casson's Spitfire Mk VB, W3458, east of Marquise on 9 August 1941. The centre section was destroyed when the pilot deliberately ignited the port-fire device.

SPITFIRE

Pilots of 118 Squadron with a Spitfire Mk VB at Ibsley in Hampshire – note the rubber condom-like sleeve over the cannon barrel, to keep the barrel dirt-free.

In 1942, the classic and highly successful British wartime film *First of the Few* was released – a morale boosting romanticised interpretation of the story of R.J. Mitchell, the Schneider Trophy and birth of the Spitfire. The film was directed by Leslie Howard, who starred in the film with David Niven. This poster is from the film's United States release – where it was re-titled simply *Spitfire*.

SPITFIRE: THE ICONIC FIGHTER IN UNIQUE PHOTOGRAPHS

One of the scenes featured an airfield under attack and a crash-landing – performed here by the CO of 118 Squadron, Squadron Leader Frank Howell. Howard directs from the wrecked Spitfire's cockpit, whilst Howell, hands on hips, considers the scene with sun-glasses wearing Niven. This is yet another presentation aircraft, Mk VB P8789. It was not really destroyed, though it was on 1 June 1942, when Flight Sergeant Ron Stillwell abandoned the machine over the Channel due to engine failure. Fortunately the pilot was rescued from the water after two hours by a 277 Squadron Walrus – also designed by R.J. Mitchell.

Left: Lesley Howard on set at Ibsley with a 118 Squadron Spitfire Mk IIA.

Opposite: Howard in conversation with 118 Squadron's Flight Lieutenant Peter Howard-Williams, one of the pilots involved in flying for the cameras.

SPITFIRE

SPITFIRE: THE ICONIC FIGHTER IN UNIQUE PHOTOGRAPHS

A 118 Squadron Mk IIA, 'Sinaboong', P8376, at Ibsley in 1941. This Spitfire was destroyed in a mid-air collision over Hampshire later that year.

Flight Lieutenant Peter Howard-Williams of 118 Squadron, sat on wing, with members of his flight and personal Mk IIA, named after his girlfriend 'Shelia'. All of this pilot's Spitfire's were also adorned with a black labrador's head silhouette within a white box – this can just be seen beneath the windscreen.

A less well-known and unsung Spitfire role was photographic reconnaissance, the pilots flying unarmed machines to save weight and increase performance, their motto being 'Unarmed and unafraid'.

More anonymous but essential groundcrew feeding the guns of a Spitfire Mk VB.

SPITFIRE: THE ICONIC FIGHTER IN UNIQUE PHOTOGRAPHS

Fighter Command's offensive daylight operations over northern France in 1941 were often complex operations involving hundreds of aircraft. These are the Spitfire Mk Vs of Northolt's Polish fighter wing taking off on one such operation that fateful year.

Pilot Officer Stanisław Wandzilak of 308 Squadron prepares for an offensive sweep. The Polish marking was usually painted on the engine cowling, but appears here in an unusual location.

The Polish Pilot Officer Stanisław Stabrowski of 308 (City of Kraków) Squadron at Northolt in 1941, his Spitfire accommodating the national insignia in the usual place.

SPITFIRE: THE ICONIC FIGHTER IN UNIQUE PHOTOGRAPHS

A 308 Squadron Spitfire Mk VB returns to Northolt safely.

A Spitfire taking hits over France in June 1941.

SPITFIRE

Above and below: Cannon-fire damage to the tail of Spitfire Mk VB, ZF-J, which Sergeant Jan Okroj of 308 Squadron safely returned to Northolt on 20 September 1941.

Pilot Officer Roger Boulding of 74 Squadron, pictured at Gravesend in spring 1941 with Spitfire P8394, 'Gibraltar'.

Pilots of 74 Squadron at Gravesend with Spitfire Mk IIA P8388, 'Black Vanities'.

An uncaptioned photograph from the album of 74 Squadron pilot Bob Poulton, the serial number of this aircraft, either a Mk IA or, more likely, a Mk VA, obscured by the personnel posing with the Spitfire. The aircraft has obviously been forced-landed.

Another Poulton snapshot: a spitfire practising deck landings on HMS *Argus* in 1941.

A Spitfire Mk VB of the Czech 310 Squadron being refuelled from a bowser.

A Spitfire Mk VC of 310 Squadron, 'trolly accumulator' plugged in. The stub adjacent to the cannon was to facilitate fitting an extra weapon.

Spitfire Mk VCs of 310 Squadron taxi for take-off.

Spitfire Mk V engine installation, Castle Bromwich Aeroplane Factory.

SPITFIRE: THE ICONIC FIGHTER IN UNIQUE PHOTOGRAPHS

Another busy factory producing Spitfires and the naval Seafire version was Westland Aircraft at Yeovil.

Above: Factory-fresh Spitfires aligned outside Westland Aircraft in 1942.

Opposite: The Free French also flew Spitfires: Squadron Leader Bernard Duperier, commanding 340 'Free French' Squadron at Biggin Hill, his Spitfire showing the Cross of Lorraine to great effect.

SPITFIRE

SPITFIRE: THE ICONIC FIGHTER IN UNIQUE PHOTOGRAPHS

The nature of the air war began changing in 1942. The previous year, RAF fighters had begun flying in support of the Army in North Africa. To make the Spitfire more manoeuvrable at low level, the wing tips were removed, leading pilots to consider these aircraft 'clipped, cropped and clapped!' This is a clipped-wing Mk VB at 52 Operational Training Unit, Aston Down.

An airborne clipped-wing Spitfire Mk VB.

SPITFIRE

Right: In the Western Desert Spitfires were first used as fighter bombers. This is an early Mk V in North Africa, armed with two 250-lb bombs.

Below: Wing Commander Ian 'Widge' Gleed leading a section of Spitfires off Tunisia, his wing leader's pennant and personal initials clearly visible.

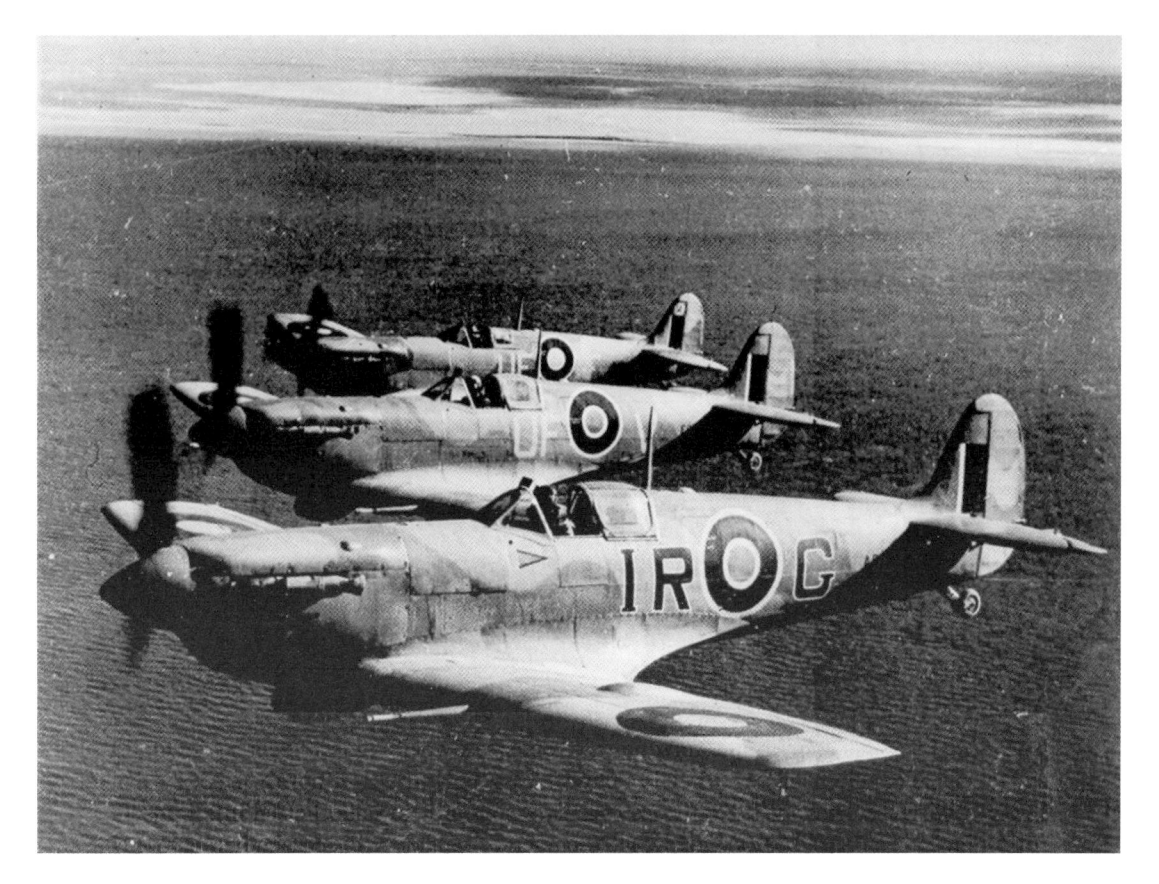

An excellent close-up of the Vokes Air Filter on a Desert Air Force Spitfire Mk V.

A Desert Air Force Mk VB taxies for take-off from a Tunisian airfield. Such airstrips were improvised, evidenced by the steamroller.

Clipped wing Spitfire Mk V in profile.

The same aircraft banks away, showing its square wingtips to great effect.

SPITFIRE: THE ICONIC FIGHTER IN UNIQUE PHOTOGRAPHS

Desert Spitfire Mk VB – captured Me 109G behind.

The Fleet Air Arm operated the carrier version of the Spitfire, the 'Seafire', with folding wings to save space and an 'arrester hook' to stop the aircraft's landing run. This Mk V is fitted with a prototype arrester hook.

SPITFIRE

The Mediterranean island of Malta was heavily besieged by Axis forces and subjected to sustained heavy air attacks. Strategically the island was crucial to operations in that theatre, so had to be held at all costs. On 7 March 1942, fifteen Spitfires eventually reached the island. This is one of them, preparing to take-off from HMS *Eagle*.

Spitfires arrived on Malta at a moment of particular crisis – sixty-four on 9 May 1942, more nine days later. Those that got in safely turned the tide of battle, amongst them these Mk Vs at Takali.

Above: This Takali Mk VB, BR130, was damaged in action on 14 October 1942, repaired and later transferred to the Americans.

Left: A Spitfire Mk VB is 'turned around' in its sand-bagged revetment. Note fuel being poured in by way of a tin can.

SPITFIRE

Emphasising the contrast in culture: a Maltese farmer and a Spitfire Mk VC.

Leading Aircraftman Maurice Leo served with 249 Squadron's groundcrew at Takali – this and the following five snapshots being taken there by him. This picture shows a wrecked Spitfire following yet another raid.

Above and below: Takali scramble!

Above and below: Maintenance, Malta style.

SPITFIRE: THE ICONIC FIGHTER IN UNIQUE PHOTOGRAPHS

No. 249 Squadron Spitfire Mk VC.

A 152 Squadron Spitfire Mk VC at Maison Blanche, Algeria, in November 1942. For a short period, the squadron used the identification letter 'L', before reverting to the usual 'UM'. This machine had previously been engaged in the ferocious Malta air battles.

Back in England, Fighter Command's front-line squadrons were all now equipped with the Spitfire Mk IX – like this aircraft of the Polish 317 Squadron. More examples of this type were produced than any other Spitfire variant, the two-stage supercharger requiring a four-bladed propeller and a nose extension of 18 inches. The increased performance was more than a match for the FW190, which had ruled the skies since ousting the Spitfire Mk V.

The menace from German high-altitude reconnaissance bombers had led to the development of the first high altitude Spitfire variant, the Mk VI, but this was essentially a Mk V and was underpowered. The Merlin 61 of the Mk IX, however, provided more opportunity, and so the Mk VII was born. With a service ceiling of 39,500 feet and a pressurised cockpit, this aircraft flew higher than ever before. Interestingly, whilst wings had been clipped for low-level operations, for high altitude work the wing tips of these Spitfires were extended – as indicated by this photograph, and the cockpit was pressurised. As the high-altitude threat passed, the Mk VII was phased out of production by 1944, 140 having been built.

SPITFIRE: THE ICONIC FIGHTER IN UNIQUE PHOTOGRAPHS

A high-flying Spitfire Mk VII at Boscombe Down – ironically, as the high-altitude threat passed, these aircraft were employed as any other Spitfire variant in 1944, including low-level ground attack.

Spitfire Mk XVIs, with tear drop canopies, being produced at Castle Bromwich.

Seafires under construction at Westland Aircraft.

SPITFIRE

Right, below and bottom: Seafires on the deck of HMS *Formidable*.

A pair of 611 Squadron Spitfire Mk IXs.

Flying Officer Robert Martin Davidson, of 222 Squadron at Hornchurch, with Spitfire Mk IX MA509 'Uruguay XVI'. This aircraft also flew with 152 Squadron in North Africa, and provided cover for the Anzio beach-head with 94 Squadron in 1944. Sadly Davidson was killed in action, on 6 April 1945, flying a Hawker Tempest Mk V.

The most successful Spitfire of all was Mk IX EN398, the personal mount of Wing Commander Johnnie Johnson, leader of the Canadian Wing at Kenley in 1943. Johnson, pictured here with that aircraft, which sports both his initials and the maple leaf insignia, destroyed twelve of his final score of thirty-eight and a half enemy aircraft destroyed, shared five and damaged five more.

SPITFIRE: THE ICONIC FIGHTER IN UNIQUE PHOTOGRAPHS

Wing Commander Johnnie Johnson aloft from Kenley in a factory-fresh Spitfire Mk IX in 1943.

Maison Blanch in Algiers became a staging point for allied aircraft pending the invasion of Sicily. This is a Spitfire Mk VC of 152 Squadron seen there soon before the invasion. Note the temporary runway surface.

On 10 July 1943, the Allies invaded Sicily, from which Mediterranean island the invasion of Italy was launched the following year. Here personnel of 152 Squadron receive a briefing concerning the dangers of malaria on Sicily. The Spitfire Mk VC sports the Desert Air Force's yellow cross motif on the engine cowling.

These are Spitfire Mk IXs, operating from a dusty airstrip, of 152 Squadron whilst supporting those campaigns. Increasingly, Spitfire pilots found themselves not mixing it with enemy fighters but engaged on ground-attack sorties.

SPITFIRE: THE ICONIC FIGHTER IN UNIQUE PHOTOGRAPHS

Spitfire Mk IXs of 43 Squadron at Catania, Sicily, 1943. The centre aircraft was that of a flight commander, Flight Lieutenant Ron Rayner DFC. The foremost aircraft shows an open hatch, providing access to flying control wires. Codes of these aircraft were red, outlined in white.

Flying in support of the advancing Allied armies, low-level attacks made aircraft vulnerable to ground fire – by 1945, Ron Rayner was commanding a flight of 72 Squadron at Ravenna and had a narrow escape when his Spitfire was holed by flak during a strafing run – 3 feet to the left and the round would have hit the pilot's seat.

A Spitfire Mk IX in the Mediterranean theatre. The pilot appears to be an American.

Ground personnel of 152 Squadron with one of their Spitfires in Sicily – the harsh environment is clearly evident.

SPITFIRE: THE ICONIC FIGHTER IN UNIQUE PHOTOGRAPHS

A Spitfire Mk VC of 152 Squadron over flies other squadron aircraft at Lentini East, on the Italian mainland in July 1943.

Above: By September 1943, 152 Squadron had re-equipped with the superior Spitfire Mk IX – seen here at Serretelle, Salerno, at that time.

Left: Wing Commander Geoffrey Page DFC, commanding 125 Wing, preparing to take-off for another ground attack sortie.

Re-organised into the Second Tactical Air Force, by 1944 the home-based Spitfire squadrons were already practising for the invasion of enemy occupied France. This would entail tactical deployment, supporting the army, flying from temporary airfields, able to move quickly and at short notice. Squadrons moved to airfields in the south of England, living in tented accommodation and with mobile workshops. Here, Wing Commander Johnnie Johnson leads his Canadians off, in a clipped-wing Spitfire LF Mk IX, from Lashenden.

A 222 Squadron pilot poses with his damaged Spitfire Mk IX in early 1944, captioned 'Don't argue with the front-end of a 190' in Squadron Leader Bob Beardsley's album.

SPITFIRE: THE ICONIC FIGHTER IN UNIQUE PHOTOGRAPHS

Significantly, in 1944 a new generation of Spitfires appeared, powered by the Rolls-Royce Griffon engine. This is the Seafire version.

Spitfire Mk IVX. Note, again, the clipped wing for low-level work.

SPITFIRE

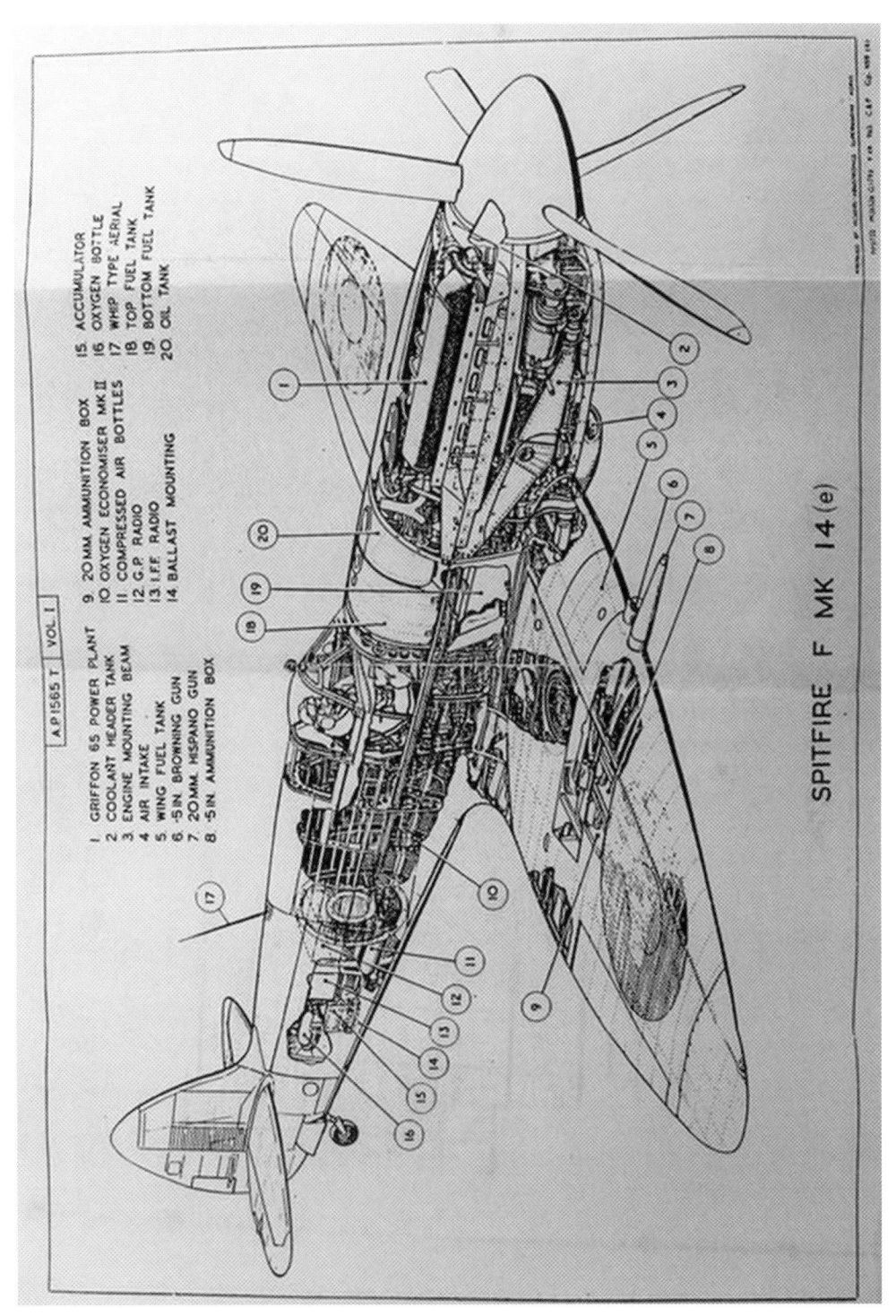

A contemporary plan from Pilot's Notes of the Spitfire F Mk IVXE – an almost entirely different shape to the early Merlin-engined Spitfires.

SPITFIRE: THE ICONIC FIGHTER IN UNIQUE PHOTOGRAPHS

The Allied air forces assembled a huge number of aircraft with which to assault Hitler's 'Fortress Europe'. To assist with identification, Allied machines were given black and white stripes. Here a Canadian Spitfire has its 'war paint' applied at Tangmere on 5 June 1944, the day before D-Day. The rough and ready application is noteworthy.

A Spitfire Mk IVX complete with 'D-Day stripes'.

SPITFIRE

The Allies landed on the beaches of Normandy on 6 June 1944. The appended air operation was enormous. Here, a wing of Spitfire Mk IXs, fitted with auxiliary fuel tanks, patrol over the beaches.

Soon, Spitfires were operating from cornfields in Normandy.

Above, below and opposite above: Spitfires being serviced in the field, during the Normandy campaign.

Below: Flight Lieutenant Kazek Budzik of 308 (Polish) Squadron with his bombed-up Spitfire Mk IX on 29 October 1944. Minutes later, Budzik strafed an enemy staff car but was shot down by flak near the Dutch Breda-Dortrecht Bridge. He forced-landed and was back in action almost immediately.

Budzik's ZF-A after his crash-landing. On 6 November 1944, he fell victim to flak again whilst strafing a train – and walked away from a forced-landing near Gorinchem.

The Griffon-engined mount of Wing Commander Johnnie Johnson, pictured in Germany, 1945. This engine required a five-bladed propeller.

Spitfires also served in the Far East. After fighting up Sicily and Italy, 152 Squadron joined Allied air forces in the Far East. There their Spitfires sported this impressive black panther artwork – and note the small fuselage roundel common to that theatre.

Warrant Officer Jimmy Chuck (right) and groundcrew of 152 Squadron at Tamu, Burma, in 1944.

No. 152 Squadron's Warrant Officer John Vickers, Tamu, 1944.

A 152 Squadron Spitfire Mk VIII at Tamu, 1944.

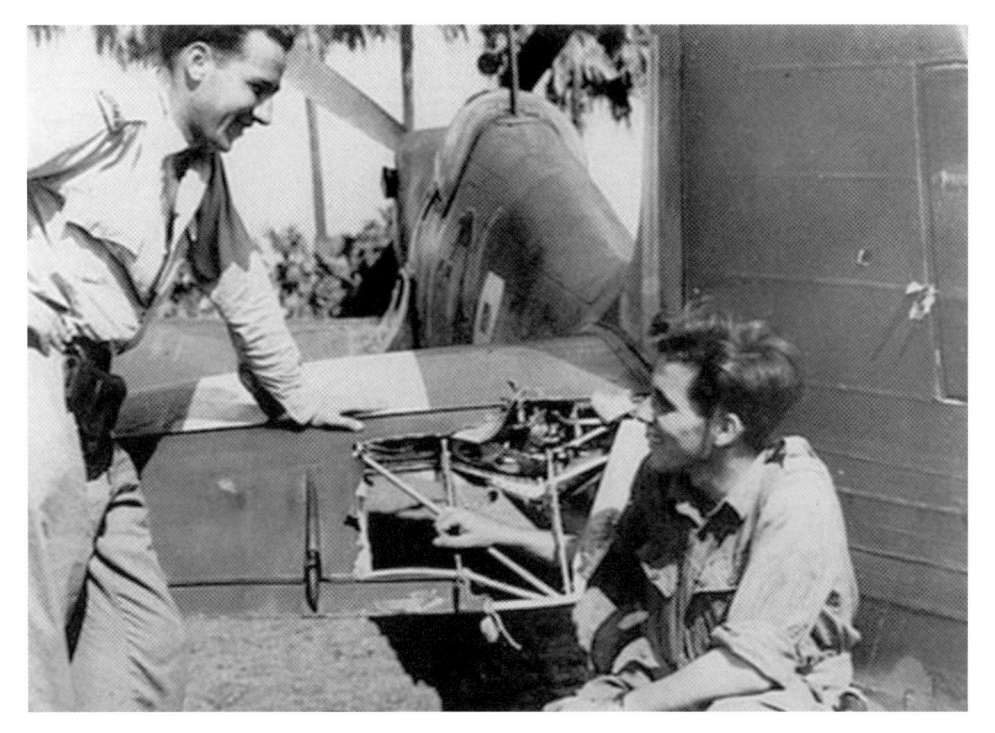

Burma, 1945: Warrant Officers Ron 'Birdie' Partridge (left), an Australian member of 152 Squadron, and Cyril Potter contemplating the damage to the latter's Spitfire – caused by a Japanese 'Oscar'.

No. 152 Squadron's black panther chases 81 Squadron's Ace of Spades.

SPITFIRE: THE ICONIC FIGHTER IN UNIQUE PHOTOGRAPHS

This snapshot of a Spitfire Mk IX clearly showing the enlarged air intake required for the two-stage Merlin, and a 'slipper' auxiliary fuel tank. The aircraft is airborne over India in 1945.

The war in Europe, of course, ended on 8 May 1945, but continued to rage in the Far East – 152 Squadron's Sergeant 'Titch' Sheppard (left) and Flight Sergeant 'Flash' Fenton, 'B' Flight's 'Chiefy', are pictured at Sinthe, Burma, with a Spitfire Mk VIII, in 1945, before the cessation of hostilities with Japan.

Above and below: Home in England, at Hamble, near Southampton, wrecked Spitfire Mk IXs, all with D-Day markings and mostly from Canadian squadrons, are unceremoniously scrapped.

The Second World War concluded with Japan's surrender on 15 August 1945. These Spitfires, including 'UM-C', flown by 152 Squadron's CO, Squadron Leader G. Kerr, were snapped in a new post-war world – Tengah, late 1945.

In the Far East too, there were Spitfire graveyards, one being visited here in 1945 by Squadron Leader Laurence 'Rubber' Thorogood DFC and friends. The Spitfires are Mk VIIIs.

Above and overleaf pages: Spitfire development continued after the Second World War, the final variant being the Griffon-engined Mk 24. The last RAF front-line fighter squadron to operate the Spitfire was 80 Squadron, based at Kai Tak, Hong Kong until 1952. The following ten snapshots show the arrival of 80 Squadron's Mk 24s in Hong Kong.

SPITFIRE: THE ICONIC FIGHTER IN UNIQUE PHOTOGRAPHS

SPITFIRE

SPITFIRE: THE ICONIC FIGHTER IN UNIQUE PHOTOGRAPHS

SPITFIRE

SPITFIRE: THE ICONIC FIGHTER IN UNIQUE PHOTOGRAPHS

SPITFIRE

Reflections

After the Second World War, the Spitfire's fighting days were not, in fact, over. Spitfires saw active service in the subsequent Malayan Emergency and Korea, and, having been sold to both the Egyptian and Israeli air forces, Spitfire even fought Spitfire over the Middle East. Finally, in 1957, the Spitfire made its last operational flight with the RAF before becoming a museum piece in a world dominated by new jet aircraft.

The Spitfire's contribution to the Allied war effort, however, was not just limited to the world's battlegrounds. The Spitfire gripped the public imagination in a way no other aircraft has ever achieved before or since. In 1940, for example, so-called 'Spitfire Funds' swept the free world, patriotic citizens raising cash for Spitfires – although very small numbers of other aircraft types were 'presented' to the government in this way, the public's preference for and pre-occupation with the Spitfire was apparent from this phenomenon. Before and during the war, of course, it was necessary to generate confidence in the Spitfire, for the public to believe that here was the wonder weapon that would save Britain from the dreaded German bombers. Consequently a myth was soon woven around the Spitfire, one which has since been maintained and re-worked over time. Today the Spitfire has evolved into a symbol of British national pride and superiority, harking back to the glory days of Empire and Total Victory in the Second World War. Today, getting on for a century after the Spitfire first flew, an increasing number of Spitfires are still being restored to airworthiness, delighting air show crowds, and two-seater variants and conversions even provide flight experiences for those so inclined to fly a Spitfire from the backseat. Indeed, the Spitfire truly remains alive and well in British popular culture and is an important icon in Britain's national identity.

One thing is certain: there has never been another aircraft as uniquely inspirational as the Spitfire, partly because the Spitfire story is inexorably connected with that of 1940 – the one year that encapsulates everything about British greatness. Hopefully Spitfires will continue to grace our more peaceful skies for many years to come. What, I wonder, would R.J. Mitchell think, to know not only how much his Spitfire contributed to victory in the Second World War, but equally that, getting on for a century after it first flew, the story of his little fighter is still far from over?

Acknowledgements

All of the survivors who have contributed to my research over the years have my enduring thanks – none, sadly, are alive today.

As ever, my friend and commissioning editor, Martin Mace, and the team at Pen & Sword were a pleasure to work with.

Select Bibliography

Boot, H. and Sturtivant, R., *Gifts of War: Spitfires and Other Presentation Aircraft in Two World Wars*, first edition, Air-Britain, Tonbridge, 2005

Mitchell, G. and MItchell, R.J., *World Famous Aircraft Designer: From Schooldays to Spitfire*, first edition, Nelson & Saunders, Olney, 1986

Morgan, E. and Shacklady, E., *Spitfire: The History*, first edition, Key Publishing, Stamford, 1987

Price, A., *The Spitfire Story*, second edition, Arms & Armour, London, 1995

Other Books by Dilip Sarkar

Spitfire Squadron: No. 19 Squadron at War, 1939–41
The Invisible Thread: A Spitfire's Tale
Through Peril to the Stars: RAF Fighter Pilots Who Failed to Return, 1939–45
Angriff Westland: Three Battle of Britain Air Raids Through the Looking Glass
A Few of the Many: Air War 1939–45, A Kaleidoscope of Memories
Bader's Tangmere Spitfires: The Untold Story, 1941
Bader's Duxford Fighters: The Big Wing Controversy
Missing in Action: Resting in Peace?
Guards VC: Blitzkrieg 1940
Battle of Britain: The Photographic Kaleidoscope, Volumes I–IV
Fighter Pilot: The Photographic Kaleidoscope
Group Captain Sir Douglas Bader: An Inspiration in Photographs
Johnnie Johnson: Spitfire Top Gun, Part I
Johnnie Johnson: Spitfire Top Gun, Part II
Battle of Britain: Last Look Back
Spitfire! Courage & Sacrifice
Spitfire Voices: Heroes Remember
The Battle of Powick Bridge: Ambush a Fore-thought
Duxford 1940: A Battle of Britain Base at War
The Few: The Battle of Britain in the Words of the Pilots
Spitfire Manual 1940
The Sinking of HMS Royal Oak *in the Words of the Survivors* (re-print of Hearts of Oak)

OTHER BOOKS BY DILIP SARKAR

The Last of the Few: Eighteen Battle of Britain Pilots Tell Their Extraordinary Stories
Hearts of Oak: The Human Tragedy of HMS Royal Oak
Spitfire Voices: Life as a Spitfire Pilot in the Words of the Veterans
How the Spitfire Won the Battle of Britain
Spitfire Ace of Aces: The True Wartime Story of Johnnie Johnson
Douglas Bader
Fighter Ace: The Extraordinary Life of Douglas Bader, Battle of Britain Hero (re-print of above)
Spitfire: The Photographic Biography
Hurricane Manual 1940
River Pike
The Final Few: The Last Surviving Pilots of the Battle of Britain Tell Their Stories
Arnhem 1944: The Human Tragedy of the Bridge Too Far
Spitfire! The Full Story of a Unique Battle of Britain Fighter Squadron
Battle of Britain 1940: The Finest Hour's Human Cost
Letters from The Few: Unique Memories of the Battle of Britain
Johnnie Johnson's 1942 Diary: The War Diary of the Spitfire Ace of Aces
Johnnie Johnson's Great Adventure: The Spitfire Ace of Ace's Last Look Back
Sailor Malan – Freedom Fighter: The Inspirational Story of a Spitfire Ace
Spitfire Ace of Aces – The Album: The Photographs of Johnnie Johnson
The Real Spitfire Pilot, being the previously unpublished original manuscript of *Spitfire Pilot,* by Flight Lieutenant David Crook, with introduction, commentary and photographs by Dilip Sarkar
Bader's Big Wing Controversy: Duxford 1940
Bader's Spitfire Wing: Tangmere 1941
Spitfire Down: Fighter Boys Who Failed to Return
Forgotten Heroes of The Battle of Britain
Faces of The Few
Spitfire Faces
Arise to Conquer: The Real Hurricane Pilot by Wing Commander Ian Gleed, introduction, commentary and photographs by Dilip Sarkar

Free French Spitfire Hero: The Diaries of and Search for René Mouchotte (with Jan Leeming)

I Had A Row with a German by Group Captain Tom Gleave, introduction by Dilip Sarkar

Battle of Britain: The Finest Hour in Cinema

Battle of Britain: The Movie (contributor to and publisher of the now late Robert Rudhall's original edition (2000), and editor and substantial contributor to 2022 revised edition)

Faces of HMS Royal Oak*: The 'Mighty Oak' Disaster at Scapa Flow*

Battle of Britain Volume 1: The Gathering Storm – Prelude to the Spitfire Summer of 1940

Battle of Britain Volume 2: The Breaking Storm – 10 July 1940–12 August 1940

Battle of Britain Volume 3: Attack of the Eagles – 13 August 1940–18 August 1940

Battle of Britain Volume 4: Airfields Under Attack – 19 August 1940– 6 September 1940

Battle of Britain Volume 5: Target London – 7 September 1940–17 September 1940

Battle of Britain Volume 6: Daylight Defeat – 18 September 1940– 30 September 1940

Battle of Britain Volume 7: The Final Curtain – 1 October 1940–31 October 1940

Battle of Britain Volume 8: The Battle of Britain Remembered

A Spitfire's Story – The Invisible Thread: Spitfire R6644 and the Pilots Who Flew It